RICARDO
Slow Cooker Favourites

Ricardo: Slow Cooker Favourites
Original French-language edition copyright © 2012 by Les Éditions La Press Ltée. All rights reserved.
English-language translation copyright © 2013 HarperCollins Publishers Ltd. All rights reserved.

Published by HarperCollins Publishers Ltd, by arrangement with Les Éditions La Press Ltée, Montréal, Québec, Canada.

Originally published in French under the title "La mijoteuse" by Les Éditions La Press Ltée, Montréal, Québec, Canada: 2012

First published in English by HarperCollins Publishers Ltd in this hardcover edition: 2013

Editorial director: Martine Pelletier
Project editor: Brigitte Coutu
Author: Ricardo Larrivée
Art director: Sonia Bluteau
Recipe writers: Kareen Grondin, Étienne Marquis
Photography: Christian Lacroix
Food styling: Anne Gagné
Prop styling: Sylvain Riel
Graphic design: Geneviève Larocque
Illustrations: Rodolphe Thuaud
Photography assistant: Pierre-Alain Faubert
Photographs of Ricardo: Dominique Lafond

HarperCollins books may be purchased for educational, business, or sales promotional use through our Special Markets Department.

HarperCollins Publishers Ltd
2 Bloor Street East, 20th Floor
Toronto, Ontario, Canada
M4W 1A8

www.harpercollins.ca

Library and Archives Canada Cataloguing in Publication information is available

ISBN 978-1-44342-405-9

Printed and bound in Canada

RICARDO

Slow Cooker Favourites

FROM LASAGNA TO CRÈME BRÛLÉE

Ricardo Larrivée

Translated by Claudia M. Theriault

HarperCollins*Publishers*Ltd

Falling in love

+++ I steered clear of the slow cooker for years. It was of no interest to me. I found the very idea of using a slow cooker about as exciting as boiling water. Slow cooking reminded me of my dear old aunt's dinner offerings in the 1970s: brown, tasteless, and just plain boring.

So why am I publishing my very own slow cooker recipe book? What has happened? Is this what it has come to? And what next? My best toaster recipes, perhaps?

More than six million slow cookers are sold every year in North America. I constantly receive requests for slow cooker recipes. So I decided to be a little more open-minded, take a closer look, and do some investigating.

We put four slow cookers to use in my test kitchen, and for an entire year my team and I studied the possibilities from every conceivable angle. The advantages of using a slow cooker quickly became clear, and I discovered plenty of useful tricks.

The slow cooker reminds me somewhat of the microwave oven. We were all crazy about it when it first appeared on the market; it was going to revolutionize the way we cooked. There would be no need for conventional ovens anymore because everything could be cooked in the microwave. Well, with time and trials, we realized that such was not the case, especially when it came to dealing with the Christmas turkey. Still, we did not get rid of our microwaves, did we. They are very useful time savers. The same applies to slow cookers.

It is important to me that anything cooked in a slow cooker be as flavourful and appealing as if it had been cooked in a conventional oven. That's why every recipe in this book is guaranteed to come out just right. They have been tested numerous times and have proved to me that the slow cooker is an ideal cooking tool. +++

RICARDO

Contents

Discover

DUST OFF YOUR SLOW COOKER

Does your slow cooker hark back to the days of Woodstock? It hasn't gone out of style—on the contrary. Dust it off and remove the *Peace and Love* decal. It'll be as good as new. Rumour has it that John Lennon had a slow cooker on his night table at the Queen Elizabeth Hotel during his bed-in with Yoko Ono in 1969! How could he have stayed in bed that long otherwise? So have your very own bed-in and slow cook your latest recipe from the comfort of your bedroom.

TESTS AND MORE TESTS

Although some books tell us that everything can be slow cooked, I do not agree. Certain dishes simply do not turn out right when they're slow cooked. As I was writing this book, I kept asking myself the same questions: Why would I make this in a slow cooker? What's the advantage?

Several recipes did not turn out well, such as bread, cakes, risotto, and moussaka (too many steps, no browning, too moist, unappetizing). I realized that the slow cooker is great for simmered dishes, for cooking with a sauce, for tenderizing tougher cuts of meat, and, surprisingly enough, for a number of desserts that are conventionally cooked in a double boiler or in an even moist heat, such as crème caramel and pudding cakes.

When we were testing, we sometimes turned the slow cooker on just before going to bed. Baked beans or ham seemed like a good idea. Night cooking, however, is not for the faint of heart. Waking to the smell of cooked onions is not my idea of a good start to the day. I much prefer the enticing aroma of coffee.

There were various mishaps as well during our testing period, such as power outages and my teenager unplugging the slow cooker to plug in an iPod!

Should there be a power outage or an accidental unplugging of your appliance, it's usually best to throw out the contents of the slow cooker and start again from scratch. If you suspect that the slow cooker has not been off too long, use a thermometer to check the temperature of the contents. If it's over 60°C (140°F), transfer the contents to an ovenproof skillet and continue cooking in a conventional oven. Avoid turning the slow cooker back on once it has shut off. It could take forever for your dish to get back to the desired temperature, so you could risk food contamination.

PRACTICAL IT'S PERFECT FOR BUSY PEOPLE. WHETHER YOU ARE STUCK IN A TRAFFIC JAM, ON THE SLOPES, OR AT YOUR YOUNGEST ONE'S HOCKEY GAME, THE SLOW COOKER IS TAKING CARE OF DINNER. YOU COME HOME TO THE AROMA OF A NICE HOT MEAL. DINNER IS READY WHEN YOU ARE READY. A SOLUTION TO THE WORK-TIME VERSUS FAMILY-TIME DILEMMA. **ECONOMICAL** IT'S WONDERFUL FOR TENDERIZING CHEAPER AND TOUGHER CUTS OF MEAT. AFTER SLOW COOKING, MEAT LITERALLY MELTS IN YOUR MOUTH. INEXPENSIVE LEGUMES AND ROOT VEGETABLES COOK PERFECTLY IN A SLOW COOKER. **HEALTHY** SLOW COOKING IS GENERALLY VERY HEALTHY BECAUSE IT IS RECOMMENDED TO USE LESS FATTY CUTS OF MEAT AND SKINLESS POULTRY. IT'S AN EASY COOKING METHOD FOR LEGUMES. AND BECAUSE IT IS OFTEN SUGGESTED THAT YOU ADD VEGETABLES TO THE DISH, IT IS A ONE-POT MEAL. **ECOLOGICAL** IT USES ABOUT AS MUCH ENERGY AS A 100-WATT LIGHT BULB.

Getting acquainted

If you want to eat well and make no effort to do so, there are two possible solutions: **go to a restaurant or believe in miracles!** The first solution is not very practical, and the second one is unusual. Between the two is the slow cooker. **It won't do all the work for you, but it will do most of it,** as long as you start the cooking process properly.

The **secret to flavourful dishes:** take the time to brown the meat and the vegetables before placing them in the slow cooker. Colouring the ingredients in this way involves what is called the Maillard reaction, which enhances all the flavours. As meat cannot brown in a slow cooker, this step is essential to almost every recipe if you want to obtain a wonderfully delicious dish that is never boring.

Cooking time may vary depending on the power of your appliance, the size of the ingredients used, and the starting temperature of the food. So you should learn how to use your slow cooker and adapt these recipes according to its power. If your slow cooker cooks a little faster or a little slower than average, adjust the cooking time—especially for recipes like pudding cakes, brownies, steamed salmon, and omelettes. The more often you use your slow cooker, the better the results.

POWER TEST You can do the following test to become familiar with your slow cooker's power level. Fill it three-quarters full with water, cover with the lid, and warm it on low for 4 hours. The water temperature should then be between 90 and 95°C (195 and 205°F). If the temperature is higher, then you will know that your slow cooker is quicker than average, and you can adjust the suggested cooking time accordingly. If, however, the temperature is lower than 90°C, your cooking time will be longer than the recipes suggest.

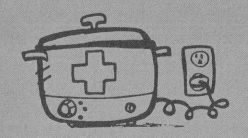

SAFE THE SLOW COOKER IS NOT A FIRE HAZARD AND DOES NOT CAUSE FOOD CONTAMINATION. THE DANGER ZONE FOR BACTERIA DEVELOPMENT IS BETWEEN 4 AND 60°C (40 AND 140°F); HOWEVER, SLOW COOKERS REACH TEMPERATURES HIGH ENOUGH TO **DESTROY BACTERIA.** WHEN THE APPLIANCE IS ON LOW, FOOD TEMPERATURE REACHES ABOUT 90°C (200°F), JUST UNDER THE POINT AT WHICH WATER BOILS. EVEN WHEN THE APPLIANCE IS SET TO WARM, THE INSIDE TEMPERATURE IS **ABOVE THE DANGER ZONE** AT ABOUT 74°C (165°F). IT IS BEST NOT TO LIFT THE LID TOO OFTEN, ESPECIALLY WHEN COOKING ON LOW, BECAUSE A GOOD DEAL OF HEAT IS LOST EACH TIME AND THE SLOW COOKER CAN TAKE UP TO 20 MINUTES TO GET BACK TO THE DESIRED TEMPERATURE.

5 things
YOU SHOULD KNOW BEFORE COOKING

1. All the recipes in this book were developed in 6-quart (5.6 L) oval slow cookers.

2. The slow cooker allows you to cook on low or on high heat. High is twice as fast as low, so you should remember that 1 hour of cooking on high equals 2 hours of cooking on low. The appliance's temperature varies between 90°C/200°F (low) and 150°C/300°F (high).

3. For best results, most recipes, except for desserts, should be cooked on low. If you want to cook on high to save time, you can, but the end result could be different.

4. Each slow cooker recipe has a circle on the page that lets you know if the dish can be kept on warm. But remember that keeping food on warm for any great length of time may change its texture, its taste, and its appearance.

5. Because the heating elements are located on the sides of the appliance, not on the bottom, there is no need to stir during cooking to prevent sticking.

the everyday
slow cooker

When I was a kid, it was really nice to come home after school to the wonderful aroma of a dinner my mother had prepared during the day. Today, with both parents working, that is a rarity. But the slow cooker can become a "time machine" and offer twenty-first-century youngsters a similar experience. Place your ingredients in the slow cooker in the morning, and by the time you get home in the evening, the aroma of a delicious family meal will greet your children just as it did for so many people back in the seventies. The only thing missing would be for the slow cooker to say, "OK, kids, now turn off the TV and do your homework!"

recipes for busy people

pineapple chicken

PINEAPPLE CHICKEN

WARM YES

Preparation 25 MINUTES   *Cook* 4 H 30   *Serves* 4 TO 6   *Freezes well*

There is very little evaporation in slow cooking, so you don't need to add a lot of liquid. Recipes like this one may appear at first to be lacking in liquid, but during cooking, the condensation under the lid will trickle down into the cooker to make the sauce. The pineapple juice makes for a lovely sauce.

Sauce

15 mL (1 tbsp) cornstarch
60 mL (1/4 cup) chicken broth
30 mL (2 tbsp) brown sugar
30 mL (2 tbsp) ketchup
30 mL (2 tbsp) soy sauce
30 mL (2 tbsp) rice vinegar
30 mL (2 tbsp) pineapple or apricot jam

Chicken

1 kg (2 lb) skinless, boneless chicken thighs, cut in half
30 mL (2 tbsp) olive oil
500 mL (2 cups) fresh pineapple cut into 1 cm (1/2-inch) pieces
4 green onions, thinly sliced (white and green parts separate)
15 mL (1 tbsp) finely chopped fresh ginger
2 cloves garlic, chopped
1 red bell pepper, seeded and diced
250 mL (1 cup) sugar snap peas cut into 3 pieces
Salt and pepper

1 SAUCE In a bowl, dissolve the cornstarch in the broth. Add the remaining ingredients and mix thoroughly. Set aside.

2 CHICKEN In a large skillet over high heat, brown the chicken in the oil a few pieces at a time. Season with salt and pepper. Transfer the chicken to the slow cooker as it browns.

3 In the same skillet, brown the pineapple, the white part of the green onions, and the ginger. Add oil if needed. Add the garlic and continue cooking for 1 minute. Deglaze with the sauce and simmer for 1 minute. Pour onto the chicken. Cover and cook on low for 4 hours.

4 Add the bell pepper, sugar snap peas, and green part of the green onions. Mix thoroughly. Continue cooking, covered, on low for about 30 minutes. (If the chicken was kept on warm, bring the cooker up to high before adding the vegetables. Allow about 45 minutes for them to cook.) Adjust the seasoning.

5 Serve with rice. Do not stir the chicken once it is cooked, as it tends to fall apart or shred.

WHOLE CHICKEN AND CHICKEN BROTH

Preparation 15 MINUTES   ***Cook*** 8 HOURS   ***Quantity broth*** 2.5 L (10 CUPS)
Quantity cooked chicken 1.25 L (5 CUPS)   ***Freezes well***

This is a winning formula, two meals in one. What simmers for today's dinner gives us a head start on tomorrow's meal—homemade chicken broth for soup or a risotto, for example.

2 carrots, peeled and cut into pieces
2 stalks celery, cut into pieces
1 onion, peeled and quartered
1 clove
2.5 mL (1/2 tsp) peppercorns
2 bay leaves
1 chicken (1.6 kg/3-1/2 lb), skin removed
Salt

1 In the slow cooker, combine the vegetables and the spices. Place the chicken on top and cover with cold water up to 5 cm (2 inches) from the edge. Season lightly with salt. Cover and cook on low for 8 hours.
2 Remove the chicken and set it aside on a plate. Let it cool to room temperature before deboning it. Strain the broth through a sieve.
3 Both the chicken and the broth can be kept in the refrigerator for 3 to 4 days and in the freezer for up to 6 months.

whole chicken

RECIPE P31

chicken broth

BEEF AND CHICKPEA SOUP

Preparation 25 MINUTES   *Soak* 12 HOURS   *Cook* 6 HOURS
Serves 6   *Freezes well*

When the family's schedule starts to look like NASA's, Houston, we have a problem ... Perhaps a good solution to the work-time versus family-time dilemma is to get out the slow cooker. It's an excellent way to rediscover homemade cooking without having to be at the stove all day.

375 mL (1-1/2 cups) dried chickpeas
454 g (1 lb) stewing beef or blade roast, diced
30 mL (2 tbsp) butter
2 onions, thinly sliced
3 cloves garlic, finely chopped
1.5 L (6 cups) beef or chicken broth
15 mL (1 tbsp) tomato paste
15 mL (1 tbsp) soy sauce
10 mL (2 tsp) harissa
1 L (4 cups) tightly packed baby spinach
Salt and pepper

1 Place the chickpeas in a large bowl. Cover with water and let soak overnight at room temperature. Add water if needed so the chickpeas are always submerged. Rinse and drain.
2 In a large skillet, brown the meat in the butter. Season with salt and pepper. Transfer to the slow cooker.
3 In the same skillet, brown the onions. Add butter if needed. Add the garlic and cook for 1 minute. Transfer to the cooker and add the chickpeas and the remaining ingredients, except for the spinach. Mix thoroughly. Season with salt and pepper.
4 Cover and cook on low for 6 hours or until the chickpeas are tender. Add broth if needed. Add the spinach 5 minutes before serving. Adjust the seasoning.

BEEF STROGANOFF

Preparation 30 MINUTES   *Cook* 4 HOURS   *Serves* 4   *Freezes well*

If you plan on using the leftover beef Stroganoff another time, add yogurt only to the amount you will be eating right away. The next day, heat up the meat and add the yogurt just before serving, so the sauce does not curdle.

675 g (1-1/2 lb) beef sirloin, cut into strips
45 mL (3 tbsp) all-purpose flour
45 mL (3 tbsp) olive oil
2 onions, thinly sliced
454 g (1 lb) white button mushrooms, sliced
45 mL (3 tbsp) butter
3 cloves garlic, chopped
125 mL (1/2 cup) red wine
250 mL (1 cup) beef broth
15 mL (1 tbsp) whole-grain mustard
2.5 mL (1/2 tsp) paprika
180 mL (3/4 cup) plain 10% yogurt
Flat-leaf parsley, finely chopped
Fresh chives, finely chopped
Salt and pepper

1 In a bowl, dredge the meat in the flour.
2 In a large skillet over high heat, brown the meat in the oil in small batches. Season with salt and pepper. Transfer the meat to the slow cooker as it browns.
3 In the same skillet, brown the onions and mushrooms in the butter. Season with salt and pepper. Add the garlic and cook for 1 more minute. Deglaze with the wine. Transfer to the cooker. Add the remaining ingredients, except for the yogurt and fresh herbs. Mix thoroughly.
4 Cover and cook on low for 4 hours.
5 When ready to serve, stir in the yogurt and adjust the seasoning. Serve on a bed of egg noodles and sprinkle with the fresh herbs.

LASAGNA

Preparation 30 MINUTES   *Cook* 4 HOURS   *Serves* 6

This lasagna, cooked entirely in the slow cooker, has become a classic at our house. And don't be afraid to use uncooked pasta. It really works, you'll see. Beware: do not use precooked lasagna noodles for this recipe.

454 g (1 lb) Italian sausage meat, mild or spicy (about 4 sausages)
1 large carrot, peeled and finely grated
1 stalk celery, finely chopped
115 g (4 oz) white button mushrooms, finely chopped
2 cloves garlic, finely chopped
1 L (4 cups) homemade or store-bought tomato sauce
12 uncooked lasagna noodles (approx.)
250 mL (1 cup) grated Parmigiano-Reggiano cheese
1 container (475 g) ricotta cheese
375 mL (1-1/2 cups) grated mozzarella cheese
Salt and pepper

1 In a bowl, combine the meat, carrot, celery, mushrooms, and garlic. Season with salt and pepper. Set aside.
2 In the bottom of the slow cooker, spread 125 mL (1/2 cup) of tomato sauce. Cover with a layer of lasagna noodles. Break them if needed so they fit.
3 Spread one-third of the meat mixture over the noodles. Cover with 250 mL (1 cup) of tomato sauce and sprinkle with 75 mL (1/3 cup) of Parmesan. Cover with another layer of lasagna noodles. Cover with the ricotta cheese.
4 Continue with a layer of lasagna noodles. Add another third of the meat mixture.
5 Cover with another layer of noodles, the remaining meat mixture, 250 mL (1 cup) of tomato sauce, and the remaining 150 mL (2/3 cup) of Parmesan. Top with the remaining tomato sauce and sprinkle with the mozzarella cheese.
6 Cover and cook on low for 4 hours. Cooking time may vary depending on the type of slow cooker you have. If the pasta is tender when a knife is inserted, the lasagna is ready. Try not to leave the lasagna on warm after it is cooked because the pasta will get soggy.

FLEMISH CARBONNADE

Preparation 25 MINUTES   *Cook* 5 HOURS   *Serves* 4
Freezes well

Flemish carbonnade, a traditional beer and beef stew from Belgium, has been one of my favourite dishes for a long time. I love it with mashed potatoes or puréed cauliflower.

1 kg (2 lb) flank steak, cut into 4 pieces
30 mL (2 tbsp) olive oil
4 large onions, thinly sliced
30 mL (2 tbsp) butter
30 mL (2 tbsp) all-purpose flour
1 bottle (341 mL) red, golden, or dark beer
125 mL (1/2 cup) chicken broth
30 mL (2 tbsp) brown sugar
30 mL (2 tbsp) balsamic vinegar
15 mL (1 tbsp) Dijon mustard
Salt and pepper

1 In a large skillet, brown the meat in the oil. Season with salt and pepper. Transfer to the slow cooker. Set aside.
2 In the same skillet, brown the onions in the butter. Season with salt and pepper. Dust with the flour and mix thoroughly. Add the beer and bring to a boil while stirring. Transfer to the cooker and add the remaining ingredients. Mix thoroughly.
3 Cover and cook on low for 5 hours. Adjust the seasoning.
4 Serve with mashed potatoes.

LAYERED "STUFFED" CABBAGE

Preparation 20 MINUTES   *Cook* 4 HOURS   *Serves* 4

You get all the flavour of cabbage rolls without having to do any rolling. Cabbage, beef, rice, and tomatoes—we didn't forget a thing.

340 g (3/4 lb) Toulouse or Italian sausage, casings removed
340 g (3/4 lb) ground beef
1 large onion, finely chopped
3 cloves garlic, finely chopped
10 mL (2 tsp) dry mustard
5 mL (1 tsp) celery salt
5 mL (1 tsp) dried oregano
125 mL (1/2 cup) uncooked parboiled long-grain rice
1 can (796 mL/28 oz) diced tomatoes
2 L (8 cups) thinly sliced cabbage
180 mL (3/4 cup) chicken broth
Salt and pepper

1 In a bowl, combine the sausage meat, ground beef, onion, garlic, and spices. Season with salt and pepper.
2 In the slow cooker, crumble half of the meat mixture. Spread half the rice and a third of the tomatoes over the meat. Cover with half the cabbage and press down lightly. Season with salt and pepper.
3 Cover with the remaining meat and rice. Pour in another third of the tomatoes and cover with the remaining cabbage. Press down lightly. Season with salt and pepper. Pour in the remaining tomatoes and the broth. Cover and cook on low for 4 hours.

WARM MAXIMUM 2 HOURS

BOLOGNESE SAUCE

Preparation 25 MINUTES   *Cook* 8 HOURS   *Quantity* 2 L (8 CUPS)
Freezes well

During regular cooking, evaporation helps concentrate all the flavours of the ingredients. Because there is very little evaporation with a slow cooker, we have to add extra-flavourful ingredients for good results. Tomato paste is one of them. Soy sauce works well in other recipes to enhance the flavour. For a Bolognese sauce, it is essential to brown the meat before placing it in the slow cooker. No shortcuts!

115 g (1/4 lb) pancetta, finely chopped
1 kg (2 lb) ground meat (mix of veal, pork, and beef)
30 mL (2 tbsp) olive oil
2 onions, finely chopped
2 carrots, peeled and grated
2 stalks celery, finely chopped
3 cloves garlic, finely chopped
125 mL (1/2 cup) red or white wine
1 can (796 mL/28 oz) crushed tomatoes
180 mL (3/4 cup) chicken broth
180 mL (3/4 cup) milk or 35% cream
1 can (156 mL/5.5 oz) tomato paste
2 bay leaves
Salt and pepper

1 In a large skillet, brown the pancetta and ground meat in the oil, making sure you crumble the ground meat. Season with salt and pepper. Transfer to the slow cooker.
2 In the same skillet, brown the onions, carrots, celery, and garlic. Add oil if needed. Season with salt and pepper. Deglaze with the wine and reduce for about 1 minute. Transfer to the cooker.
3 Add the remaining ingredients and mix thoroughly. Cover and cook on low for 8 hours. Remove the bay leaves and adjust the seasoning. Let rest for a while and then stir well, so the liquid on the surface blends into the sauce.
4 Serve over pasta and sprinkle generously with shaved Parmesan.

date and lemon
chicken tajine

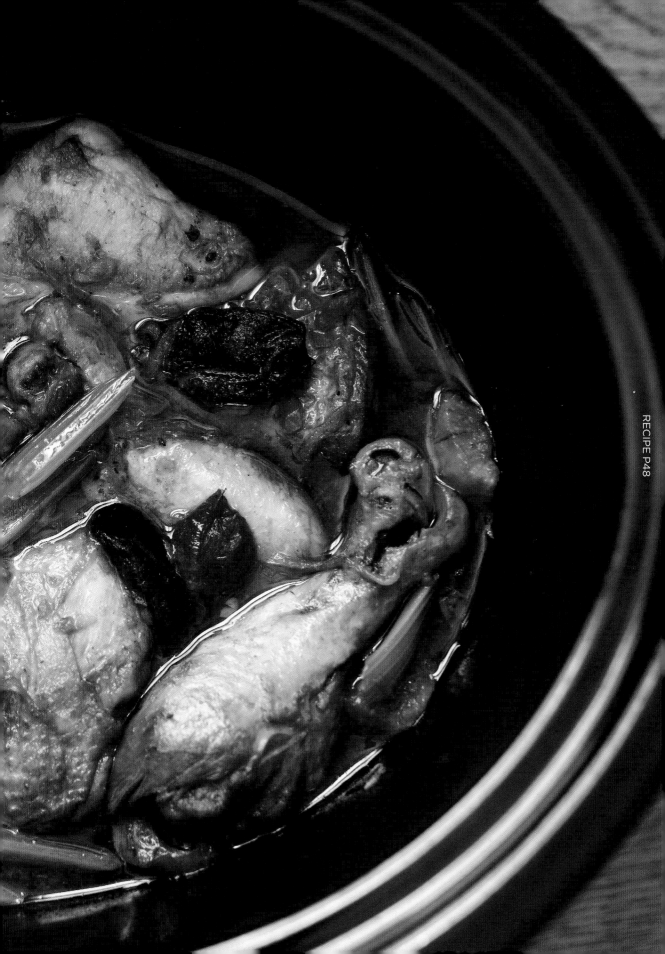

RECIPE P48

DATE AND LEMON CHICKEN TAJINE

Preparation 30 MINUTES   *Cook* 4 HOURS   *Serves* 6   *Freezes well*

Both the tajine and the slow cooker operate on the same basic principle: simmer slowly, with very little fat, and let the steam rise and trickle back down to produce a flavourful sauce.

1 chicken (1.4 kg/3 lb), cut into 8 pieces (or 4 thighs and 4 drumsticks, bone-in)
60 mL (1/4 cup) olive oil
1 onion, thinly sliced
2 cloves garlic, chopped
5 mL (1 tsp) ground coriander
2.5 mL (1/2 tsp) ground cumin
2.5 mL (1/2 tsp) ground ginger
2.5 mL (1/2 tsp) ground turmeric
250 mL (1 cup) chicken broth
1 sweet potato, peeled and cut into large cubes
2 stalks celery, sliced diagonally
2 tomatoes, quartered
6 Medjool dates, pitted and quartered
Peel of 1 preserved lemon (or of 1/4 well-washed fresh lemon), finely diced
30 mL (2 tbsp) finely chopped flat-leaf parsley
30 mL (2 tbsp) finely chopped fresh cilantro
Salt and pepper

1 In a large skillet, brown the chicken in half the oil. Season with salt and pepper. Transfer to the slow cooker.
2 In the same skillet, brown the onion in the remaining oil. Season with salt and pepper. Add the garlic and spices and cook for 1 minute. Add the broth and bring to a boil. Transfer to the cooker. Add the remaining ingredients, except for the fresh herbs.
3 Cover and cook on low for 4 hours. Add the fresh herbs and adjust the seasoning.
4 Serve with couscous.

PORK CHILI

Preparation 30 MINUTES   *Soak* 12 HOURS   *Cook* 8 HOURS
Serves 4 TO 6   *Freezes well*

Chili is perfect in the slow cooker. You can easily adapt your own chili recipe by following this method and the amount of liquid given.

250 mL (1 cup) dried red beans
454 g (1 lb) skinless, boneless pork shoulder, cut into 2.5 cm (1-inch) cubes
30 mL (2 tbsp) olive oil
340 g (3/4 lb) lean ground beef
1 large onion, finely chopped
1 jalapeño pepper, seeded and finely chopped
2 cloves garlic, finely chopped
15 mL (1 tbsp) cocoa powder
30 mL (2 tbsp) chili powder
15 mL (1 tbsp) paprika
1 mL (1/4 tsp) ground cumin
1 mL (1/4 tsp) cayenne pepper
1 can (796 mL/28 oz) diced tomatoes
250 mL (1 cup) chicken broth
Salt and pepper

1 Place the beans in a bowl. Cover with water and let soak overnight at room temperature. Add water if needed so the beans are always submerged in water. Rinse and drain.
2 In a large skillet, brown the pork in the oil, half at a time. Season with salt and pepper. Transfer to the slow cooker.
3 In the same skillet, brown the ground beef. Add oil if needed. Season with salt and pepper. Transfer to the cooker.
4 In the same skillet again, sauté the onion, jalapeño, garlic, cocoa, and spices for about 3 minutes. Add oil if needed. Transfer to the cooker. Add the tomatoes and broth. Cover and cook on low for 8 hours. Adjust the seasoning, adding extra cayenne pepper to taste.
5 Serve over rice, with corn chips, or as a filling for baked potatoes.

RECIPE P52

meatloaf

MEATLOAF

Preparation 30 MINUTES   *Cook* 5 HOURS   *Serves* 4 TO 6   *Freezes well*

My mother-in-law has always cooked her meatloaf in the oven—like most of us, actually. But then I asked myself, "Why not try it in the slow cooker?" The result was a pleasant surprise. All that's left to do when you get home is to make some mashed potatoes.

Sauce
125 mL (1/2 cup) ketchup
1 onion, coarsely chopped
1 clove garlic, coarsely chopped
15 mL (1 tbsp) Worcestershire sauce
Salt and pepper

Meatloaf
340 g (3/4 lb) ground pork
340 g (3/4 lb) ground beef
20 salted crackers (saltines), crushed
2 eggs
15 mL (1 tbsp) Worcestershire sauce
10 mL (2 tsp) chili powder
5 mL (1 tsp) dry mustard
1 mL (1/4 tsp) garlic powder
250 mL (1 cup) chicken broth

1 SAUCE In a blender, purée all the ingredients until smooth. Season with salt and pepper. Set aside.

2 MEATLOAF In a bowl, combine all the ingredients, except for the broth. Season with pepper.

3 With your hands, shape the meat into a loaf about 25 x 8 cm (10 x 3 inches) and place in the slow cooker. Pour the broth all around the meatloaf. Pour the sauce over the meatloaf. Cover and cook on low for 5 hours or until a thermometer inserted in the meatloaf reads 70°C (160°F).

4 Slice and serve with mashed potatoes and a green vegetable.

GOULASH

Preparation 30 MINUTES   *Cook* 6 HOURS   *Serves* 6   *Freezes well*

Inexpensive cuts of meat turn out beautifully in the slow cooker. The blade roast in this recipe is a good example. At $3.10 per serving, it is cheaper than going to a restaurant.

1 kg (2 lb) boneless beef blade roast, cut into large cubes
45 mL (3 tbsp) butter
3 onions, cubed
3 cloves garlic, finely chopped
30 mL (2 tbsp) paprika
7.5 mL (1-1/2 tsp) ground caraway
2.5 mL (1/2 tsp) smoked paprika
60 mL (1/4 cup) all-purpose flour
500 mL (2 cups) beef broth
30 mL (2 tbsp) ketchup
30 mL (2 tbsp) balsamic vinegar
125 mL (1/2 cup) sour cream
60 mL (1/4 cup) finely chopped flat-leaf parsley
Salt and pepper

1 In a large skillet, brown the meat in the butter, half at a time. Season with salt and pepper. Transfer to the slow cooker.
2 In the same skillet, brown the onions. Add oil if needed. Add the garlic and spices and cook for 1 minute. Dust with the flour and cook for 1 more minute. Add the broth and bring to a boil, stirring constantly. Transfer to the cooker. Add the ketchup and vinegar. Mix thoroughly.
3 Cover and cook on low for 6 hours. Adjust the seasoning.
4 Serve with egg noodles or potatoes. Add a large dollop of the sour cream and garnish with the parsley.

pork satay

RECIPE P56

PORK SATAY

Preparation 30 MINUTES   *Cook* 4 HOURS   *Serves* 4 TO 6

In Indonesia, satay means a skewer of meat that has been marinated with spices and peanuts. Obviously skewers can't be grilled in a slow cooker, but this dish tastes exactly the same.

1 kg (2 lb) skinless, boneless pork shoulder, cubed
45 mL (3 tbsp) olive oil
2 cloves garlic, finely chopped
6 green onions, thinly sliced (white and green parts separate)
15 mL (1 tbsp) finely chopped peeled fresh ginger
375 mL (1-1/2 cups) chicken broth
60 mL (1/4 cup) lime juice
60 mL (1/4 cup) soy sauce
15 mL (1 tbsp) honey
10 mL (2 tsp) sambal oelek
180 mL (3/4 cup) peanut butter
125 mL (1/2 cup) plain 10% yogurt
125 mL (1/2 cup) finely chopped fresh cilantro
60 mL (1/4 cup) chopped roasted peanuts
Salt and pepper

1 In a large skillet, brown the pork in the oil, half at a time. Season with salt and pepper. At the end of browning, add the garlic and the white part of the green onions and continue cooking for about 2 minutes. Transfer to the slow cooker. Add the ginger, broth, lime juice, soy sauce, honey, and sambal oelek. Mix thoroughly.
2 Cover and cook on low for 4 hours.
3 Just before serving, remove 250 mL (1 cup) of the cooking juices from the cooker and pour it into a bowl. Add the peanut butter and whisk thoroughly. Pour this mixture into the cooker and add the green part of the green onions. Stir and adjust the seasoning. Serve over basmati rice and garnish with a dollop of the yogurt. Sprinkle with the cilantro and peanuts.

SALSA VERDE PORK TACOS

Preparation 20 MINUTES   *Cook* 8 HOURS   *Serves* 6
Pork freezes well

Store-bought salsa verde in a jar is usually fairly hot. To please the kids, we can mix some green salsa with some mild red salsa.

Pork
1.4 kg (3 lb) skinless, boneless pork shoulder, cut into 4 or 5 pieces
1 jar (450 mL/16 oz) green salsa
Salt and pepper

Tacos and garnishes
Taco shells or tortillas
Orange cheddar cheese, grated
Iceberg lettuce, thinly sliced
Tomatoes, diced
Sour cream
Mild or hot salsa

1 PORK In the slow cooker, place the pieces of pork and cover with the salsa. Season with salt and pepper. Cover and cook on low for 8 hours.
2 With two forks, pull the pork apart, removing all fat. Adjust the seasoning. Transfer the pork to a serving dish with some of the cooking juices.
3 TACOS Place the serving dish with the meat in the centre of the table, along with the taco shells and the garnishes.

58

WARM
MAXIMUM
4 HOURS

CHICKEN CACCIATORE

Preparation 30 MINUTES   *Cook* 4 HOURS   *Serves* 4   *Freezes well*

We found that adding a small amount of instant tapioca to certain dishes with sauce, like chicken cacciatore, produces a beautiful texture. A very good reason to take the little red box out of the pantry.

12 skinless chicken drumsticks or thighs
60 mL (1/4 cup) olive oil
225 g (8 oz) white button mushrooms, quartered
1 onion, thinly sliced
4 cloves garlic, finely chopped
180 mL (3/4 cup) red wine
2 red bell peppers, seeded and cubed
1 can (398 mL/14 oz) diced tomatoes
45 mL (3 tbsp) tomato paste
20 mL (4 tsp) instant tapioca
2.5 mL (1/2 tsp) celery salt
125 mL (1/2 cup) finely chopped flat-leaf parsley
Salt and pepper

1 In a large skillet, brown the chicken in half the oil. Season with salt and pepper. Transfer the chicken to the slow cooker.
2 In the same skillet, brown the mushrooms and onion in the remaining oil. Season with salt and pepper. Add the garlic and cook for 1 more minute. Deglaze with the red wine. Pour onto the chicken. Add the peppers, tomatoes, tomato paste, tapioca, and celery salt. Mix thoroughly.
3 Cover and cook on low for 4 hours. Add the parsley and adjust the seasoning.
4 Serve with egg noodles.

BEEF AND CARROT STEW

Preparation 30 MINUTES *Cook* 8 HOURS *Serves* 6 *Freezes well*

For this classic dish with a twist, we added carrot juice. You can find it in the fruit and vegetable aisle. I like the hint of sweetness it adds to the stew. When cooking potatoes in a slow cooker, make sure they are completely covered in liquid or they'll turn grey.

8 carrots, peeled and cut into 2.5 cm (1-inch) pieces
1 L (4 cups) baby potatoes, halved
500 mL (2 cups) carrot juice
1 boneless beef blade roast (about 1 kg/2 lb), cut into 6 pieces
60 mL (1/4 cup) butter
2 onions, cut into thin wedges
4 cloves garlic, finely chopped
30 mL (2 tbsp) all-purpose flour
250 mL (1 cup) beef broth
Salt and pepper

1 In the slow cooker, combine the carrots, potatoes, and carrot juice. Season with salt and pepper. Set aside.
2 In a large skillet, brown the meat in half the butter. Season with salt and pepper. Transfer to the cooker.
3 In the same skillet, brown the onions in the remaining butter. Add the garlic and cook for 1 minute. Dust with the flour and stir while cooking. Deglaze with the broth and bring to a boil, stirring constantly. Transfer to the cooker.
4 Cover and cook on low for 8 hours. Adjust the seasoning.

the slow cooker
even in summer

It is a well-known fact in my family that a slow cooker equals comfort and well-being during the long winter months. It permeates the house with wonderful aromas; it sends subliminal messages of calm and security; it promises tasty pleasures that are most welcome during the lengthy cold season. And yet summertime is when the slow cooker can really shine. At times, it can even replace the beloved barbecue. Because unlike the barbecue, the slow cooker can be used inside. It becomes the summertime chef's secret weapon, the chef who won't have to turn the kitchen into a sauna or sweat in front of a charcoal fire or a 150,000 BTU burner. Why not just lie back on a lounge chair with a glass of wine and let the slow cooker take care of your lime bavette steak? You'll be surprised by how much time you'll have to do other things—or nothing at all.

sunny day recipes

LIME BAVETTE ROLLS

Preparation 20 MINUTES   **Cook** 4 HOURS   **Serves** 4 TO 6
Steak freezes well

We usually grill our steak on the barbecue. In this recipe we put it directly in the slow cooker with all the seasonings and cook it for 4 hours. It's as simple as that! All that's left to do is to put the meat on the table with some nice crisp lettuce leaves and let everybody roll. It tastes of summer. Bavette steak is also sold as bib or flap steak.

Bavette steak
15 mL (1 tbsp) brown sugar
15 mL (1 tbsp) all-purpose flour
15 mL (1 tbsp) chili powder
5 mL (1 tsp) ground cumin
5 mL (1 tsp) ground coriander
1 kg (2 lb) bavette steak, cut against the grain into 5 mm (1/4-inch) thick strips
125 mL (1/2 cup) beef broth
2 green onions, finely chopped
1 jalapeño pepper, seeded and finely chopped
2 cloves garlic, chopped
1 lime, grated zest and juice
60 mL (1/4 cup) finely chopped fresh cilantro
Salt and pepper

Garnish
Boston lettuce leaves
Sour cream
1 or 2 avocados, sliced and drizzled with lemon juice
Fresh cilantro leaves

1 BAVETTE STEAK In the slow cooker, combine the brown sugar, flour, and spices. Add the remaining ingredients, except for the cilantro, and mix thoroughly. Season with salt and pepper.

2 Cover and cook on low for 4 hours. If the meat is kept on warm for a number of hours, it will become very tender and shred easily. Add the cilantro and adjust the seasoning.

3 GARNISH Place the meat and the garnishes in serving dishes and set them on the table. Everyone can top their lettuce leaves with sour cream, meat, avocado, and cilantro and then simply roll and enjoy.

STEAMED SALMON WITH FENNEL

Preparation 10 MINUTES   *Cook* 1 H 15   *Serves* 4

I can hear you saying, "Why cook salmon in a slow cooker when it is so easy to grill?" I was skeptical as well. But because the slow cooker cooks with an even, moist heat, the texture of the salmon cooked this way is absolutely divine. I have rarely tasted such moist salmon. One of the most pleasant surprises in our test kitchen.

250 mL (1 cup) vegetable broth
10 mL (2 tsp) anise liqueur (such as pastis or ouzo) (optional)
4 thick skinless salmon fillets
1/2 bulb fennel, stalks removed, thinly sliced, ideally on a mandoline
30 mL (2 tbsp) finely chopped fennel fronds
Salt and pepper

1 In the slow cooker, combine the broth and the liqueur, if using. Place the salmon fillets in the cooker and scatter the sliced fennel over them. Season with salt and pepper.
2 Cover and cook on low for about 1 hour and 15 minutes or until the salmon is just pink in the middle. Serve the salmon with the fennel and steamed rice. Garnish with the fennel fronds.

SEAFOOD AND FISH SOUP WITH FRESH HERBS

Preparation 30 MINUTES   *Cook* 4 HOURS   *Serves* 4 TO 6

Soup is such a simple thing to make. So why use the slow cooker? Because the vegetables and the broth will explode with flavour and aromas while cooking during part of the day. When you get home, you just add the fish and seafood. It's ready in 5 minutes.

2 stalks celery, sliced
2 shallots, finely chopped
30 mL (2 tbsp) butter
30 mL (2 tbsp) anise liqueur (such as pastis or ouzo)
1 bulb fennel, stalks removed, thinly sliced
500 mL (2 cups) peeled and diced russet potatoes
1 L (4 cups) fish or chicken broth
250 mL (1 cup) apple juice
225 g (1/2 lb) cod, cut into large cubes
225 g (1/2 lb) medium scallops
225 g (1/2 lb) medium shrimp, peeled and deveined
125 mL (1/2 cup) finely chopped fresh herbs to taste
(tarragon, flat-leaf parsley, chives, dill)
Lemon wedges
Salt and pepper

1 In a skillet, soften the celery and shallots in the butter. Deglaze with the liqueur. Transfer to the slow cooker. Add the fennel, potatoes, broth, and apple juice. Season with salt and pepper.
2 Cover and cook on high for 4 hours.
3 If the soup has been kept on warm for more than 1 hour, bring the cooker up to high before adding the fish and seafood. Add the fish and seafood and simmer for 3 to 5 minutes or until cooked. Add broth if needed. Adjust the seasoning.
4 Serve in soup bowls and sprinkle with the fresh herbs. Serve with lemon wedges alongside. If desired, serve with toasted bread slices spread with rouille (p69).

ROUILLE

Preparation 10 MINUTES   *Serves* 4

5 mL (1 tsp) lemon juice
A pinch saffron
3 cloves garlic, finely chopped
2 egg yolks
1 mL (1/4 tsp) salt
A pinch cayenne pepper
125 mL (1/2 cup) vegetable oil
8 slices baguette, toasted

1 In a bowl, combine the lemon juice and saffron.
2 In a mini food processor, purée the garlic, egg yolks, and lemon juice with the saffron, salt, and cayenne pepper.
3 With the motor running, slowly drizzle half the oil into the mixture. Add the remaining oil. The rouille should have the consistency of a thick mayonnaise. Adjust the seasoning. Refrigerate if necessary.
4 Serve the rouille, spread on the toasted bread slices, with the seafood and fish soup with fresh herbs (p68).

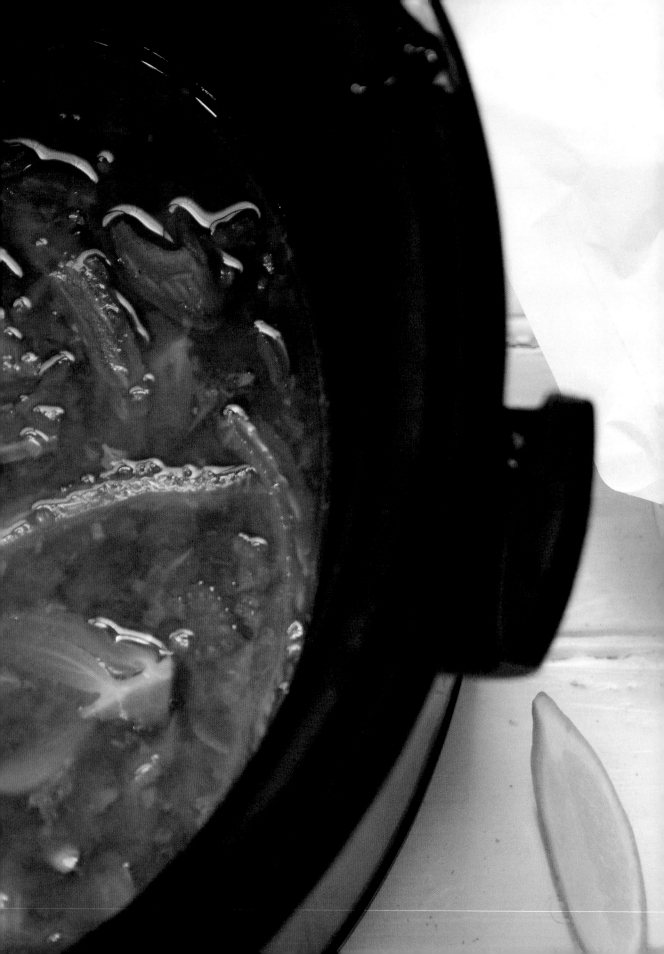

RECIPE P68

seafood and fish soup
with fresh herbs

RECIPE P68

seafood and fish soup with fresh
herbs and rouille toasts

GARDEN RATATOUILLE

Preparation 30 MINUTES   *Cook* 4 HOURS   *Quantity* 1.5 L (6 CUPS)
Freezes well

When everything in the garden grows at the same time, there are a lot of vegetables to contend with. Solution: ratatouille. It's delicious with just about everything—on pizza, on pasta, as a side dish, with an omelette. Cut all the vegetables the same size for best results.

1 small eggplant, cut into 1.5 cm (3/4-inch) cubes
2 red bell peppers, seeded and cut into strips
2 yellow zucchinis, cut into 1.5 cm (3/4-inch) thick rounds
2 green zucchinis, cut into 1.5 cm (3/4-inch) thick rounds
1 can (398 mL/14 oz) diced tomatoes
1 onion, chopped
75 mL (1/3 cup) olive oil
2 cloves garlic, chopped
2.5 mL (1/2 tsp) hot pepper flakes
15 mL (1 tbsp) sweet or smoked paprika (optional)
Salt and pepper

1 In the slow cooker, combine all the ingredients, except for the paprika, if using. Mix thoroughly. Season with salt and pepper.
2 Cover and cook on low for 4 hours. Sprinkle with the paprika, if using, and stir. Adjust the seasoning.

ORANGE-BRAISED BEET SALAD

Preparation 30 MINUTES   **Cook** 4 HOURS   **Serves** 8

I cannot get over the fact that for most of my life I've only eaten pickled beets. I never would have thought that one day I would cook them in a slow cooker. Beets are excellent vegetables, either as a side dish or as a salad. It's worth staining your hands!

Braised beets
1 kg (2 lb) whole red or yellow beets, unpeeled
2 oranges, grated zest only
500 mL (2 cups) orange juice
30 mL (2 tbsp) white wine vinegar
Salt

Vinaigrette
30 mL (2 tbsp) orange juice
30 mL (2 tbsp) white wine vinegar
5 mL (1 tsp) whole-grain mustard
5 mL (1 tsp) honey
1 small clove garlic, finely chopped
60 mL (1/4 cup) olive oil
Salt and pepper

Salad
1.5 L (6 cups) lamb's lettuce or arugula
125 mL (1/2 cup) ricotta cheese
125 mL (1/2 cup) walnuts, toasted and broken into pieces
2 oranges, peel and pith removed, cut into skinless segments
60 mL (1/4 cup) finely chopped fresh chives

1 BRAISED BEETS In the slow cooker, combine all the ingredients. Season with salt. Cover and cook on low for 4 hours. If possible, stir twice during cooking. Strain, discarding the cooking juices. Let the beets cool to room temperature, then peel them. Cut into thin wedges or cubes.

2 VINAIGRETTE In a bowl, combine all the ingredients with a whisk. Season with salt and pepper.

3 SALAD Arrange the lettuce on a platter or on individual plates and top with the beets. Garnish with dollops of the ricotta, the nuts, skinless orange segments, and chives. Drizzle with the vinaigrette.

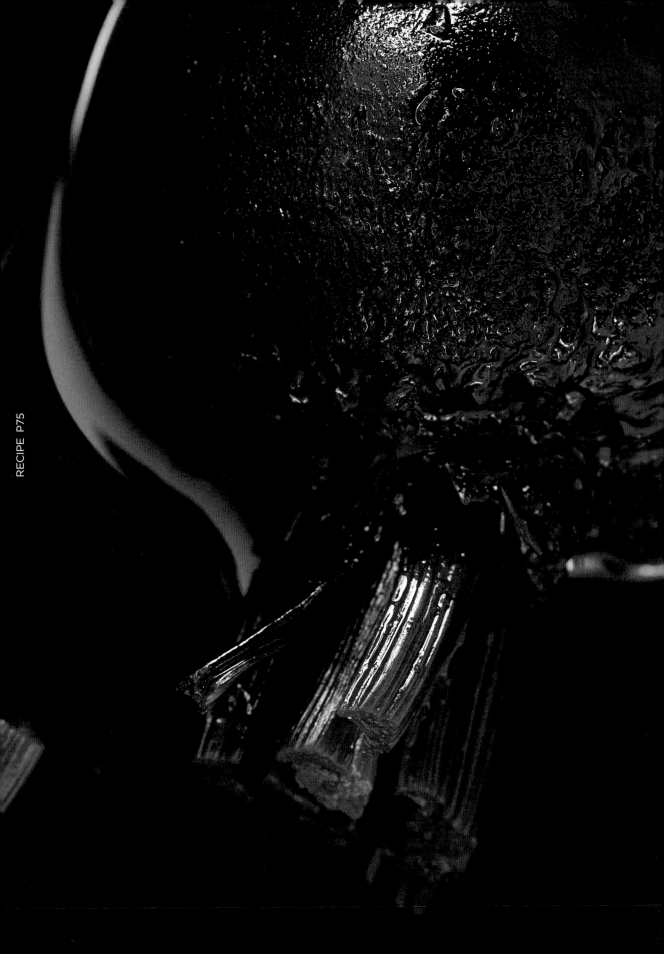

RECIPE P75

orange-braised
beet salad

BARBECUED PULLED PORK

Preparation 15 MINUTES   *Cook* 8 HOURS   *Serves* 8   *Freezes well*

The slow cooker is the perfect environment for a pork shoulder. The long cooking in barbecue sauce guarantees a very tender piece of meat that pulls apart easily with a fork. You can use this pulled pork in tacos, on corn bread, with polenta, or in a burger.

Barbecue sauce
250 mL (1 cup) ketchup
125 mL (1/2 cup) cider vinegar
125 mL (1/2 cup) apple jelly
30 mL (2 tbsp) chili powder
30 mL (2 tbsp) Dijon mustard
30 mL (2 tbsp) molasses (fancy)
30 mL (2 tbsp) Worcestershire sauce
10 mL (2 tsp) onion powder
5 mL (1 tsp) hot pepper sauce
2.5 mL (1/2 tsp) garlic powder

Roast
1 bone-in pork shoulder (about 1.8 kg/4 lb),
or 1 skinless, boneless pork roast (about 1.6 kg/3-1/2 lb)
Salt and pepper

1 SAUCE In the slow cooker, combine all the ingredients.
2 ROAST Add the meat and baste well with the sauce. Season with salt and pepper.
3 Cover and cook on low for 8 hours.
4 Remove the meat from the cooker. With a fork, pull the meat apart and set aside in a bowl.
5 Meanwhile, in a small saucepan, reduce the sauce by half. Add to the meat. Mix thoroughly and adjust the seasoning.
6 Serve in burgers (p83).

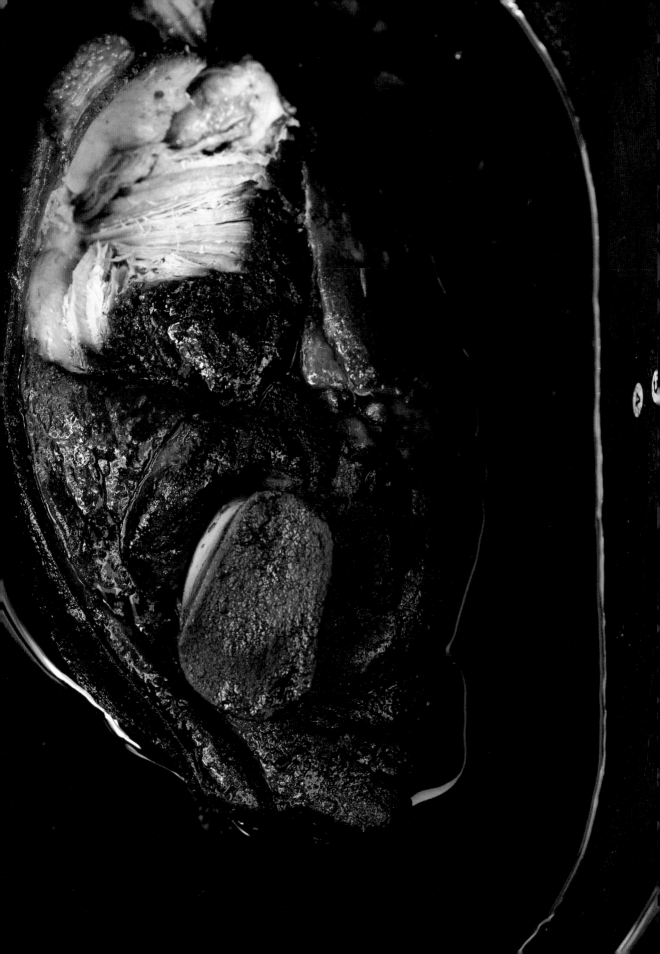

PULLED PORK BURGERS

Preparation 20 MINUTES   *Rest* 15 MINUTES   *Serves* 8

If, like me, you have had your fill of classic burgers, try pulled pork burgers with barbecue sauce. I'm sure you'll be hooked! Add a little crunchy coleslaw and you've got a superb summer dish.

Coleslaw
30 mL (2 tbsp) cider vinegar
15 mL (1 tbsp) whole-grain mustard
15 mL (1 tbsp) maple syrup
15 mL (1 tbsp) olive oil
1 apple, cored and finely julienned
1 L (4 cups) thinly sliced green cabbage
Salt and pepper

Burgers
8 large hamburger buns, toasted
750 mL (3 cups) warm barbecued pulled pork with sauce (see recipe p80)

1 COLESLAW In a large bowl, combine the vinegar, mustard, maple syrup, and oil. Add the apple and toss to coat thoroughly (to prevent browning). Add the cabbage and toss well. Season with salt and pepper. Let rest for 15 minutes.
2 BURGERS Spread the barbecued pulled pork on the bottom half of a hamburger bun and garnish with the coleslaw. Top with the other half of the bun and serve immediately.

RIBS

Preparation 20 MINUTES   **Cook** 5 HOURS   **Serves** 4

No more boiling your ribs before cooking them, with that unpleasant aroma permeating the house. When simmered directly in barbecue sauce, the ribs absorb all the flavour and become extremely tender. And the house smells wonderful. Before serving them, I grill the ribs for a couple of minutes, just to give them that special taste we love.

Barbecue sauce
180 mL (3/4 cup) ketchup
125 mL (1/2 cup) apricot jam or jelly
125 mL (1/2 cup) cider vinegar
30 mL (2 tbsp) chili powder
30 mL (2 tbsp) Worcestershire sauce
5 mL (1 tsp) onion powder
5 mL (1 tsp) garlic powder
5 mL (1 tsp) hot pepper sauce
Salt and pepper

Ribs
2 kg (4-1/2 lb) pork back ribs, cut into sections of 3 bones each

1 SAUCE In the slow cooker, combine all the ingredients. Season with salt and pepper.
2 RIBS Add the ribs and baste well. Cover and cook on low for 5 hours. The ribs should be tender but not falling off the bone. Remove the ribs from the cooker and drain.
3 Preheat the grill to high. Oil the grill rack.
4 In a small saucepan, reduce the sauce until it reaches a syrupy consistency.
5 Grill the ribs on each side, basting them with the sauce. You can also place the ribs on a baking sheet, brush them with the sauce, and broil them in the oven for a few minutes.

HONEY CHICKEN WINGS

Preparation 40 MINUTES   *Cook* 3 HOURS   *Serves* 4 TO 6

1.4 kg (3 lb) chicken wings
2 cloves garlic, finely chopped
125 mL (1/2 cup) honey
125 mL (1/2 cup) chili sauce
15 mL (1 tbsp) chili powder
15 mL (1 tbsp) Dijon mustard
10 mL (2 tsp) hot pepper sauce, or to taste
Salt and pepper

1 When preparing wings, you can see that each one has two joints. With a chef's knife, cut the wings at both joints to create three pieces from each wing. Discard the small bony tip that has no meat.
2 In the slow cooker, combine all the remaining ingredients and mix thoroughly. Add the wings and baste well. Season with salt and pepper.
3 Cover and cook on low for 3 hours.
4 Preheat the grill to medium. Oil the grill rack.
5 Remove the wings from the cooker and drain, reserving the juices. Grill for 5 to 6 minutes, basting with the cooking juices. You can also spread the wings on a baking sheet, brush them with the cooking juices, and broil them in the oven for a few minutes.
6 If desired, serve with blue cheese dip (recipe follows).

BLUE CHEESE DIP

Preparation 10 MINUTES   *Quantity* ABOUT 375 ML (1-1/2 CUPS)

125 mL (1/2 cup) mayonnaise
125 mL (1/2 cup) sour cream
125 mL (1/2 cup) crumbled blue cheese
30 mL (2 tbsp) finely chopped flat-leaf parsley
30 mL (2 tbsp) lemon juice
1 clove garlic, finely chopped
Salt and pepper

1 In a bowl, combine all the ingredients. Season with salt and pepper. Cover and refrigerate if needed.
2 Serve with the honey chicken wings.

MANGO "JAM"

Preparation 30 MINUTES   ***Cook*** 4 HOURS   ***Quantity*** 1 L (4 CUPS)
Freezes well

Making jam in a slow cooker was a great find for us. The long, slow cooking and the little amount of sugar required allowed for a nicely coloured jam with whole pieces of fruit. Because we have more control over the cooking, there is no fear of overcooking or of the jam taking on a caramelized flavour.

2 L (8 cups) peeled and finely diced mangoes
500 mL (2 cups) sugar
45 mL (3 tbsp) lemon juice

1 In the slow cooker, combine all the ingredients. Cover and cook on high for 1 hour.
2 Remove the lid and continue cooking for about 3 hours to allow the liquid to evaporate and obtain a nice thick jam. Cook longer if needed. Transfer the jam into 4 sterilized 250 mL (1-cup) jars.
3 You can keep the jam in the refrigerator for up to 2 weeks. Should you want to keep it several weeks, put the jars in the freezer.

RECIPE P93

strawberry and rhubarb "jam"

STRAWBERRY "JAM"

Preparation 30 MINUTES   ***Cook*** 4 HOURS   ***Quantity*** 1 L (4 CUPS)
Freezes well

2 L (8 cups) diced fresh strawberries
500 mL (2 cups) sugar
45 mL (3 tbsp) lemon juice

1 In the slow cooker, combine all the ingredients. Cover and cook on high for 1 hour.
2 Remove the lid and continue cooking for about 3 hours to allow the liquid to evaporate and obtain a nice thick jam. Cook longer if needed. Transfer the jam into 4 sterilized 250 mL (1-cup) jars.
3 You can keep the jam in the refrigerator for up to 2 weeks. Should you want to keep it several weeks, put the jars in the freezer.

STRAWBERRY AND RHUBARB "JAM"

Preparation 30 MINUTES   **Cook** 4 HOURS   **Quantity** 1 L (4 CUPS)
Freezes well

1 L (4 cups) diced fresh strawberries
1 L (4 cups) diced fresh rhubarb
500 mL (2 cups) sugar
45 mL (3 tbsp) lemon juice

1 In the slow cooker, combine all the ingredients. Cover and cook on high for 1 hour.
2 Remove the lid and continue cooking for about 3 hours to allow the liquid to evaporate and obtain a nice thick jam. Cook longer if needed. Transfer the jam into 4 sterilized 250 mL (1-cup) jars.
3 You can keep the jam in the refrigerator for up to 2 weeks. Should you want to keep it several weeks, put the jars in the freezer.

the slow cooker
for entertaining

Let's face it: hosting a dinner can be extremely stressful, even for a harmonious couple and those who are usually in sync. "You haven't emptied the dishwasher, and they'll be here in five minutes!" "You're not wearing that, are you?" "You forgot to cook the vegetables!" The slow cooker becomes the great equalizer: it transforms what could very well be a chaotic session of individual tasks into a project in which a couple can present a common front. Then there are those known as the "martyr cooks"—people who spend the entire evening in the kitchen, a look of total confusion on their faces. Martyr cooks are the ones whose guests, seated at the table, are often heard saying, "Where is Esther?" Thanks to the slow cooker, the host—who up until now was a slave in the kitchen—can join family and friends at the table and let the slow cooker tend to the cooking.

no-fuss recipes for entertaining

VEAL CHEEKS WITH FIGS

Preparation 30 MINUTES   **Cook** 8 HOURS   **Serves** 6   **Freezes well**

Do yourself a favour and try the wonderful piece of meat that is veal cheek. The expression "you can cut it with a fork" must have been invented for veal cheeks. You can replace two veal cheeks with one beef cheek, but the beef cheek is bigger and takes longer to cook. You must cut it into two or three pieces to cook it for the same length of time.

Veal cheeks
12 veal cheeks, trimmed of fat
60 mL (1/4 cup) butter
1 onion, chopped
45 mL (3 tbsp) all-purpose flour
625 mL (2-1/2 cups) veal stock
60 mL (1/4 cup) cognac
30 mL (2 tbsp) molasses (fancy)
12 dried figs, halved
3 stalks celery, diced
Salt and pepper

Garnish
125 mL (1/2 cup) baby arugula
1 stalk celery, thinly sliced
30 mL (2 tbsp) coarsely chopped toasted pecans

1 VEAL CHEEKS In a large skillet, brown the veal cheeks on both sides in the butter. Transfer to the slow cooker.
2 In the same skillet, soften the onion. Dust with the flour and mix thoroughly. Add the veal stock and bring to a boil, stirring constantly. Transfer to the cooker. Add the remaining ingredients. Season with salt and pepper.
3 Cover and cook on low for 8 hours.
4 GARNISH Serve the meat on a bed of puréed parsnips, puréed celery root, or mashed potatoes and garnish with the arugula, celery, and pecans.

OSSO BUCO

Preparation 40 MINUTES   *Cook* 6 HOURS   *Serves* 4   *Freezes well*

I know you are probably saying, "What? Having guests for dinner and serving them a meal from a slow cooker?" I am familiar with the prejudice. And yet . . . you can turn the slow cooker on at eleven Saturday morning, do some errands, drive the kids to their various lessons, drop in at the dry cleaner's, and everything will be ready when your guests arrive at six. What more could you ask for?

Osso buco
4 to 6 veal shanks about 5 cm (2 inches) thick
60 mL (1/4 cup) all-purpose flour
30 mL (2 tbsp) olive oil
1 onion, finely chopped
3 cloves garlic, finely chopped
250 mL (1 cup) dry white wine
60 mL (1/4 cup) tomato paste
2 stalks celery, finely chopped
2 carrots, peeled and finely chopped
250 mL (1 cup) veal stock
5 mL (1 tsp) dried thyme
Salt and pepper

Gremolata
2 lemons, grated zest only
60 mL (1/4 cup) finely chopped flat-leaf parsley
1 clove garlic, very finely chopped
Pepper

1 OSSO BUCO Dredge the veal shanks in the flour.
2 In a large skillet, brown both sides of the shanks in the oil. Season with salt and pepper. Transfer to the slow cooker.
3 In the same skillet, soften the onion and garlic. Add oil if needed. Deglaze with the wine and transfer to the cooker. Add the remaining ingredients. Mix thoroughly. Season with salt and pepper.
4 Cover and cook on low for 6 hours. Adjust the seasoning.
5 GREMOLATA In a bowl, combine all the ingredients. Arrange the osso buco on plates and sprinkle with the gremolata. Serve with pasta or mashed potatoes.

RECIPE P100

osso buco

SCALLOPED POTATOES

Preparation 30 MINUTES   ***Cook*** 5 HOURS   ***Rest*** 30 MINUTES
Serves 6

Planning a meal using only one oven can be a bit of a problem when you are having guests over. Between the roast and the dessert, there is no room in the oven to cook anything else. This is where the slow cooker saves the day—it's like having a second oven. Sometimes the finished product is even better, as is the case with scalloped potatoes. The longer it cooks, the more flavourful it becomes.

500 mL (2 cups) 35% cream
1 can (370 mL/13 oz) evaporated milk
2 cloves garlic, peeled and halved
2 L (8 cups) very thinly sliced (ideally on a mandoline) peeled russet potatoes
   (8 to 10 potatoes)
Salt and pepper

1 Butter the inside of the slow cooker.
2 In a saucepan, bring the cream, evaporated milk, and garlic to a boil. Remove from the heat, cover, and let steep for 5 minutes. Remove the garlic.
3 Line the bottom of the cooker with slices of potato. Drizzle with a little of the hot cream mixture. Season with salt and pepper. Continue alternating potatoes, hot cream, and salt and pepper until you have used all the ingredients.
4 Cover and cook on low for 5 hours. Turn the cooker off. Remove the lid and let rest for 30 minutes. If you wish to leave it on warm, you can do so for 1 hour maximum; you do not need to let it rest uncovered.

LAMB SHANKS WITH PRUNES

Preparation 30 MINUTES   *Cook* 6 TO 8 HOURS (DEPENDING ON SHANK SIZE)   *Serves* 4
Freezes well

30 mL (2 tbsp) cornstarch
250 mL (1 cup) chicken broth
20 pitted prunes, diced
30 mL (2 tbsp) balsamic vinegar
15 mL (1 tbsp) Dijon mustard
4 lamb shanks
30 mL (2 tbsp) olive oil
4 shallots, thinly sliced
2 cloves garlic, finely chopped
30 mL (2 tbsp) honey
1 star anise
250 mL (1 cup) Port wine
Salt and pepper

1 In the slow cooker, combine the cornstarch, broth, prunes, vinegar, and mustard.
2 In a large skillet, brown the shanks in the oil. Season with salt and pepper. Transfer the shanks to the cooker.
3 In the same skillet, brown the shallots. Add the garlic, honey, and star anise and cook for 1 minute, stirring constantly. Deglaze with the Port and pour into the cooker. Mix thoroughly. Season with salt and pepper.
4 Cover and cook on low for 6 to 8 hours, depending on the shank size, or until the meat is fork-tender. Adjust the seasoning.

BRAISED CARROTS

Preparation 10 MINUTES   *Cook* 4 HOURS   *Serves* 4 TO 6

30 mL (2 tbsp) butter, softened
10 to 12 carrots, peeled and halved lengthwise
250 mL (1 cup) orange juice
15 mL (1 tbsp) honey
Salt and pepper

1 Butter the bottom of the slow cooker. Place the carrots inside. Add the orange juice and drizzle with the honey. Season with salt and pepper.
2 Cover and cook on high for 4 hours or until the carrots are cooked.

lamb shanks with prunes

RECIPE P106

braised carrots

BEEF TERIYAKI

Preparation 20 MINUTES   *Cook* 4 HOURS   *Serves* 6   *Freezes well*

It is usually recommended to brown meat in a skillet before putting it in a slow cooker, to enhance the flavours. Not with this recipe, though. The sauce is particularly concentrated, so the meat ends up being incredibly flavourful.

45 mL (3 tbsp) brown sugar
30 mL (2 tbsp) cornstarch
125 mL (1/2 cup) chicken broth
1 kg (2 lb) flank steak, cut against the grain in 5 mm (1/4-inch) thick strips
125 mL (1/2 cup) ketchup
60 mL (1/4 cup) soy sauce
60 mL (1/4 cup) mirin
2 cloves garlic, finely chopped
10 mL (2 tsp) finely chopped peeled fresh ginger
2.5 mL (1/2 tsp) toasted sesame oil
2.5 mL (1/2 tsp) sambal oelek
Toasted sesame seeds
Salt and pepper

1 In the slow cooker, combine the brown sugar, cornstarch, and broth. Add the remaining ingredients, except for the sesame seeds. Season with salt and pepper. Mix thoroughly.
2 Cover and cook on low for 4 hours.
3 Serve over jasmine rice or rice vermicelli. Sprinkle with the sesame seeds.

PORT VEAL STEW

Preparation 20 MINUTES   **Cook** 8 HOURS   **Serves** 6   **Freezes well**

For a simple and chic dish, serve this with mashed potatoes or puréed cauliflower or celery root, and some brightly coloured carrots. A meal to be proud of!

1 boneless veal shoulder roast (about 1.4 kg/3 lb), not tied
15 mL (1 tbsp) olive oil
4 slices bacon, finely chopped
375 mL (1-1/2 cups) Port wine
750 mL (3 cups) small pearl onions, peeled
1 clove garlic, finely chopped
4 sprigs fresh thyme
Salt and pepper

1 In a large skillet, brown the roast in the oil. Season with salt and pepper. Add the bacon halfway through, when the roast is golden brown. Transfer the roast and bacon to the slow cooker.
2 Deglaze with the Port and pour into the cooker. Add the onions, garlic, and thyme. Cover and cook on low for 8 hours. You should be able to pull the meat apart with a fork. Adjust the seasoning. Serve with mashed potatoes.

ORANGE AND HONEY TURKEY BREAST

Preparation 30 MINUTES   **Cook** 7 HOURS   **Serves** 8   **Freezes well**

I can't even remember the number of different turkey breast recipes I have cooked in my life. I never get tired of turkey breast. I love the simplicity: no waste, no boning, and sliced turkey breast is wonderful. A no-fuss alternative for Christmas or Thanksgiving.

1 boneless turkey breast roast (2 breast halves, 1.8 kg/4 lb total),
   with or without skin, tied
45 mL (3 tbsp) butter
3 shallots, chopped
3 cloves garlic, chopped
30 mL (2 tbsp) all-purpose flour
250 mL (1 cup) chicken broth
250 mL (1 cup) orange juice
180 mL (3/4 cup) honey
1 orange, grated zest only
5 mL (1 tsp) chopped peeled fresh ginger
Salt and pepper

1 In a large skillet, brown the turkey roast on all sides in the butter. Season with salt and pepper. Transfer the roast to the slow cooker.
2 In the same skillet, soften the shallots and garlic. Dust with the flour and mix thoroughly. Add the broth and bring to a boil, stirring constantly. Pour into the cooker. Add the remaining ingredients. Season with salt and pepper.
3 Cover and cook on low for 7 hours. Slice the roast and drizzle with the cooking juices. Serve with mashed potatoes or long-grain and wild rice and a green vegetable.

orange and honey
turkey breast

RECIPE P113

RABBIT BRAISED IN RED WINE WITH PANCETTA

Preparation 25 MINUTES   *Cook* 4 HOURS   *Serves* 4 TO 6   *Freezes well*

6 rabbit legs, or a whole rabbit cut into 6 pieces
30 mL (2 tbsp) butter
1 onion, chopped
150 g (5 oz) pancetta, sliced 5 mm (1/4 inch) thick, diced
30 mL (2 tbsp) all-purpose flour
250 mL (1 cup) red wine
2 carrots, peeled and sliced or diced
1 sprig fresh thyme
250 mL (1 cup) chicken broth
15 mL (1 tbsp) tomato paste
375 mL (1-1/2 cups) cherry tomatoes, halved
60 mL (1/4 cup) coarsely chopped flat-leaf parsley
Salt and pepper

1 In a large skillet, brown the rabbit legs in the butter. Season with salt and pepper. Transfer to the slow cooker.

2 In the same skillet, brown the onion and pancetta. Dust with the flour and cook for 1 minute, stirring constantly. Deglaze with the wine and bring to a boil while stirring. Transfer to the cooker. Add the carrots, thyme, broth, and tomato paste.

3 Cover and cook on low for 4 hours. Add the tomatoes and parsley. Adjust the seasoning.

4 Serve with mashed potatoes or buttered noodles. You can also bone the meat and mix it with tagliatelle noodles and the sauce.

COQ AU VIN

Preparation 30 MINUTES   *Cook* 4 HOURS   *Serves* 4 TO 6   *Freezes well*

Removing the skin from poultry is often recommended when using the slow cooker, as it never really browns and the results are not very appetizing. However, you can keep the skin on, as its fat adds flavour, and simply discard it before serving.

6 skinless chicken legs (or 1 whole chicken, cut into pieces)
30 mL (2 tbsp) olive oil
6 slices bacon, 5 mm (1/4 inch) thick, diced
1 onion, chopped
225 g (8 oz) white button mushrooms, halved
2 cloves garlic, chopped
30 mL (2 tbsp) tomato paste
30 mL (2 tbsp) all-purpose flour
375 mL (1-1/2 cups) red wine
Salt and pepper

1 In a large skillet, brown the chicken legs in the oil. Season with salt and pepper. Transfer to the slow cooker.
2 In the same skillet, brown the bacon. Add the onion and mushrooms and cook until golden brown. Add the garlic and tomato paste and cook for 1 minute. Dust with the flour and mix thoroughly. Add the wine and bring to a boil, stirring constantly. Transfer to the cooker. Season with salt and pepper.
3 Cover and cook on low for 4 hours. Serve with rice, puréed cauliflower, or mashed potatoes.

LAMB NAVARIN

Preparation 20 MINUTES   *Cook* 6 HOURS   *Serves* 6   *Freezes well*

A great French classic that is back on my menu thanks to the slow cooker.

1 kg (2 lb) boneless lamb shoulder, trimmed of fat and cut into large cubes
45 mL (3 tbsp) all-purpose flour
24 pearl onions, peeled
60 mL (1/4 cup) butter
250 mL (1 cup) white wine
12 Nantes or other sweet new carrots, peeled
4 red potatoes, halved
750 mL (3 cups) chicken broth
30 mL (2 tbsp) tomato paste
3 sprigs fresh thyme
500 mL (2 cups) frozen peas, thawed
Salt and pepper

1 In a bowl, dredge the meat in the flour. Set aside.
2 In a large skillet, brown the onions in half the butter. Season with salt and pepper. Transfer to the slow cooker.
3 In the same skillet, brown the meat in the remaining butter. Season with salt and pepper. Deglaze with the wine and bring to a boil, stirring constantly. Transfer to the cooker. Add the carrots, potatoes, broth, tomato paste, and thyme. Mix thoroughly. Make sure the potatoes are completely covered in liquid or they'll turn grey.
4 Cover and cook on low for 6 hours. If the navarin has been kept on warm, turn the cooker to high before adding the peas. Add the peas and continue cooking for about 5 minutes. Remove the thyme sprigs. Adjust the seasoning. Serve with whole-grain mustard, if desired.

MERG
AGNE
BISO
LAPI
CER
CAN
FIB

the butcher shop

THE BEST CUTS OF MEAT FOR THE SLOW COOKER

+++ It is said that in the caves at Lascaux, they found drawings of cavemen cooking mammoth meat in a slow cooker... Joking aside, for centuries, meat has been cooked slowly in a large pot over an open fire, simmering for hours. It's not rocket science. Simmering meat has existed ever since man has had teeth and wanted to keep them intact.

TENDERIZE ONE OF THE GREAT ADVANTAGES OF A SLOW COOKER IS THAT IT OFFERS THE BEST CONDITIONS FOR TENDERIZING TOUGHER CUTS OF MEAT. SLOW COOKING ON LOW MAKES FOR MOIST HEAT, WHICH IN TURN TRANSFORMS COLLAGEN INTO GELATIN. THIS IS WHY MEAT COOKED ON LOW IS FAR MORE TENDER THAN MEAT COOKED ON HIGH. AND THE GREAT THING IS THAT TOUGHER CUTS OF MEAT ARE THE LEAST EXPENSIVE. **PERFECT CUTS** NOT ALL CUTS OF MEAT ARE IDEAL FOR THE SLOW COOKER. THE LESS TENDER PIECES ARE GOOD BRAISED OR SLOWLY SIMMERED. FOR THE MORE TENDER CUTS OF MEAT, IT IS BEST TO GRILL, SAUTÉ, OR ROAST THEM. THEY CAN TOUGHEN IN A SLOW COOKER, GIVING VERY DISAPPOINTING RESULTS.

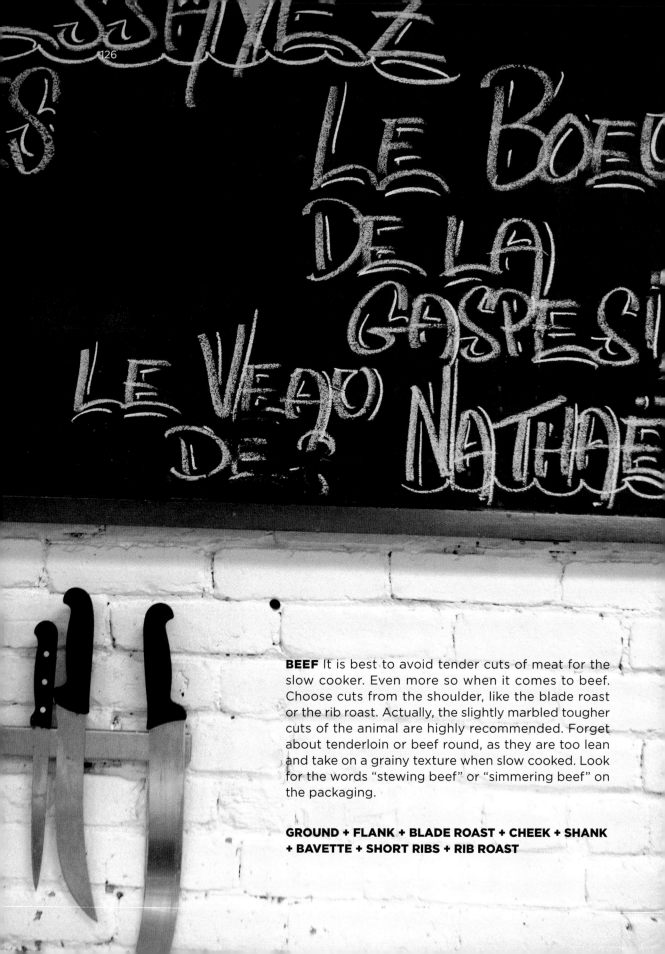

BEEF It is best to avoid tender cuts of meat for the slow cooker. Even more so when it comes to beef. Choose cuts from the shoulder, like the blade roast or the rib roast. Actually, the slightly marbled tougher cuts of the animal are highly recommended. Forget about tenderloin or beef round, as they are too lean and take on a grainy texture when slow cooked. Look for the words "stewing beef" or "simmering beef" on the packaging.

GROUND + FLANK + BLADE ROAST + CHEEK + SHANK + BAVETTE + SHORT RIBS + RIB ROAST

beef

blade

bavette

flank

lamb

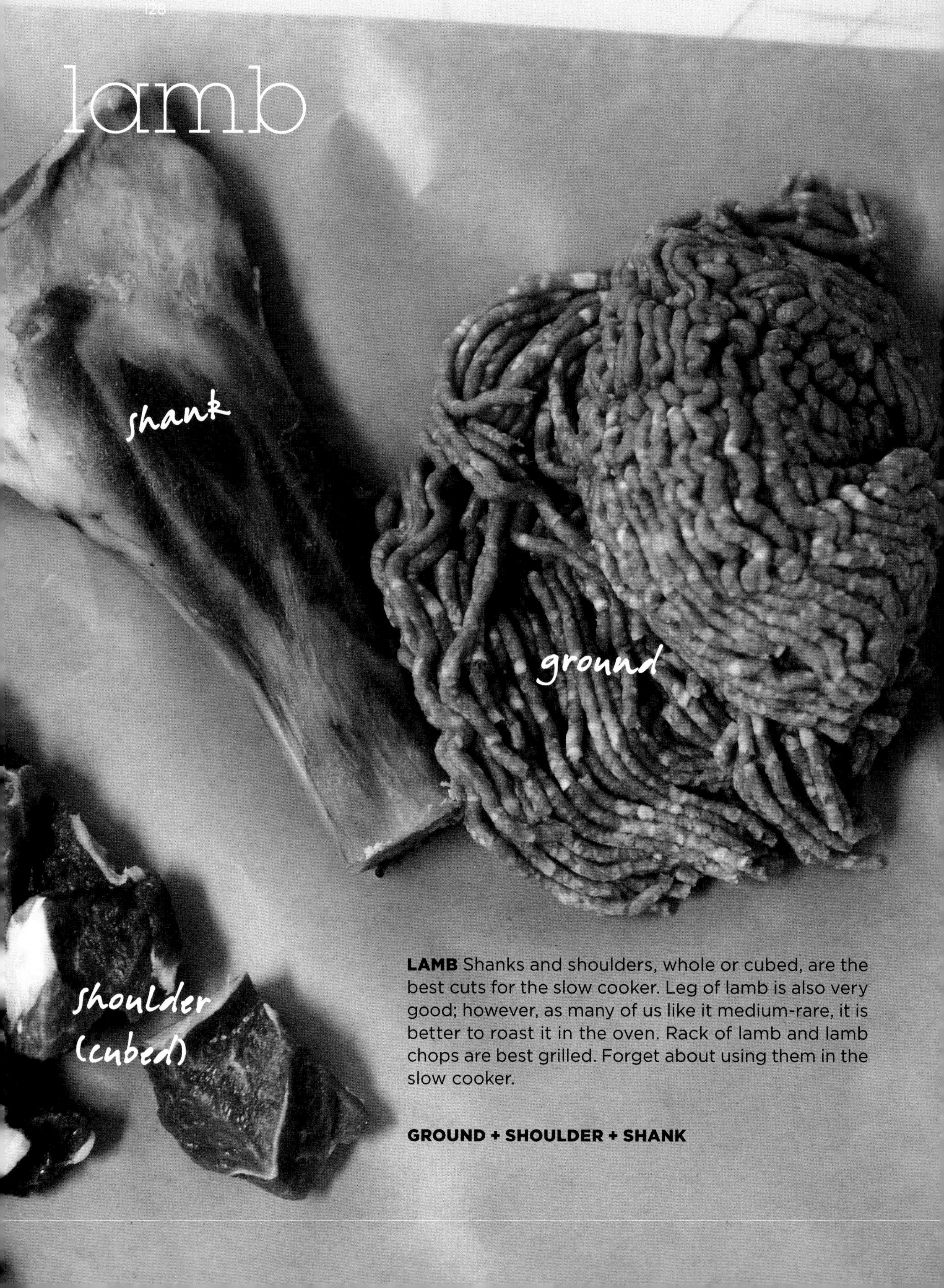

shank

ground

shoulder
(cubed)

LAMB Shanks and shoulders, whole or cubed, are the best cuts for the slow cooker. Leg of lamb is also very good; however, as many of us like it medium-rare, it is better to roast it in the oven. Rack of lamb and lamb chops are best grilled. Forget about using them in the slow cooker.

GROUND + SHOULDER + SHANK

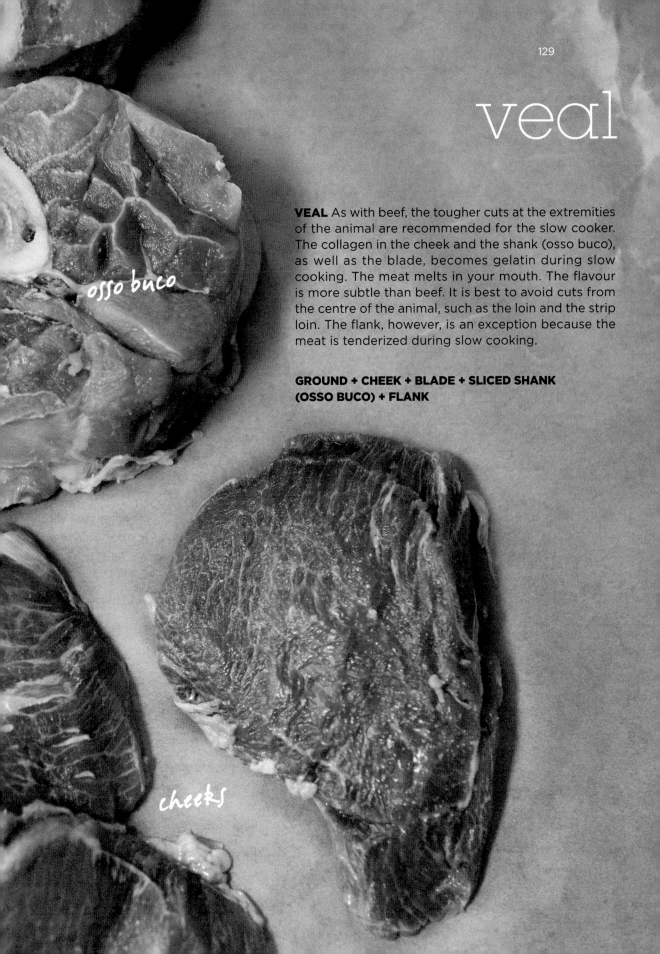

veal

osso buco

VEAL As with beef, the tougher cuts at the extremities of the animal are recommended for the slow cooker. The collagen in the cheek and the shank (osso buco), as well as the blade, becomes gelatin during slow cooking. The meat melts in your mouth. The flavour is more subtle than beef. It is best to avoid cuts from the centre of the animal, such as the loin and the strip loin. The flank, however, is an exception because the meat is tenderized during slow cooking.

GROUND + CHEEK + BLADE + SLICED SHANK (OSSO BUCO) + FLANK

cheeks

pork

ribs

osso buco

PORK Pork shoulder, when slow cooked, yields impressive results. The meat falls apart in tender morsels that we mix with sauce. Pork back ribs are also perfect. When slow cooked, there is no need to boil them first. To get that sought-after rib taste, put them on the barbecue after slow cooking them. If you can find pork cheeks, do buy them. Slow cooking transforms them into very tender meat.

GROUND + HAM + SHOULDER + RIBS + SHANK (OSSO BUCO) + SALT PORK

LARD
SALE
#12.99/1

poultry

duck leg

turkey breast

drumsticks

POULTRY Dark meat is preferable to white meat. It does not dry up as easily. One exception is turkey breast, which is quite large and does well when slow cooked. In most of our recipes, we suggest removing the skin before cooking, as it will not brown in the slow cooker. If you like, you can keep the skin on to add flavour to your dish. Just remember to remove it before serving.

WING + THIGH + TURKEY BREAST + CHICKEN, DUCK, TURKEY LEGS + DRUMSTICKS

If compliments are what you are looking for, the slow cooker is a true ally when cooking meat: "You can cut this with a fork—who needs a knife!" To which you can answer, "Of course, when one pays $40 a kilo for beef, it definitely makes a difference." Only we know it is a $10 blade roast, but we promise not to tell. +++

the sugar shack
slow cooker

The slow cooker and the sugar shack have a lot in common—people either love it or they don't. There are two camps: the "pro-maple sugar shack" and the "anti-maple sugar shack" people. Personally, I am all for it. I go every year. For me, springtime is not synonymous with budding flowers and little birds but rather with baked beans and "grand-père" maple dumplings. For those of you who profess to be part of the "anti" group, I just know there is a sugar shack fan inside you screaming to be let out. Perhaps you just have not found the right one for you—too big, too small, or too far. When you do find the right one, visiting the sugar shack becomes a regular pilgrimage. Once a year, you fast for two days so you have room for pea soup, maple-glazed ham, and maple taffy on snow. If you are part of the "pro" group and, like me, simply can't wait for that time of year, take out your slow cooker. You'll delight in all the maple syrup fare in the comfort of your own home.

recipes for sugar shack fans

PEA SOUP

Preparation 20 MINUTES   *Cook* 6 HOURS   *Serves* 6   *Freezes well*

Before making pea soup, my mother used to soak the peas and scrub them to remove the hard outer layers. Here is a version with much less work and a whole lot of taste. We chose split peas because soaking is not needed; neither is scrubbing them.

115 g (1/4 lb) streaked salt pork, without rind, diced
15 mL (1 tbsp) olive oil
1 large onion, finely chopped
2 carrots, peeled and diced
2 stalks celery, diced
375 mL (1-1/2 cups) split peas
1.5 L (6 cups) chicken broth
1 bay leaf
500 mL (2 cups) shredded cooked ham (optional)
Salt and pepper

1 In a large skillet, brown the salt pork in the oil. Add the onion and cook until tender and translucent. Transfer to the slow cooker.
2 Add the carrots, celery, split peas, broth, and bay leaf. Season with salt and pepper.
3 Cover and cook on low for 6 hours (or 8 hours for a creamier soup). Remove the bay leaf and stir in the ham, if using. Adjust the seasoning.

RECIPE P144

baked beans

BAKED BEANS

Preparation 15 MINUTES **Soak** 12 HOURS **Cook** 10 HOURS
Quantity 1.5 L (6 CUPS) **Freezes well**

Lots of people bake their beans overnight. The biggest advantage of using the slow cooker is that you don't have to get up in the middle of the night to stir them! Also, less energy is consumed than if you had the oven on all night. In the morning you can keep the beans on warm until you are ready for brunch. However, if you don't want your pyjamas to smell of beans, plug in your slow cooker in the garage to cook them!

750 mL (3 cups) dried navy beans
2 cloves
1 onion, peeled and halved
1.125 L (4-1/2 cups) chicken broth
125 mL (1/2 cup) maple syrup
115 g (1/4 lb) streaked salt pork, without rind, diced
30 mL (2 tbsp) molasses (fancy)
5 mL (1 tsp) dry mustard
Salt

1 Place the beans in a large bowl. Cover with water and let soak overnight at room temperature. Add water if needed so the beans are always submerged. Rinse and drain.
2 Stud a clove into each onion half.
3 In the slow cooker, combine all the ingredients. Cover and cook on low for 10 hours. Remove the onion and cloves. Adjust the seasoning.

MAPLE AND BEER-BRAISED HAM

Preparation 15 MINUTES   *Cook* 10 HOURS   *Serves* 10
Freezes well

WARM
YES

1 bone-in smoked ham shoulder (about 3 kg/6-1/2 lb)
30 mL (2 tbsp) Dijon mustard
3 or 4 cloves
1 bottle (341 mL) pale ale
180 mL (3/4 cup) maple syrup

1 Remove the mesh from the ham. Place the ham in the slow cooker. Brush with the mustard and stud with the cloves.
2 Add the beer and maple syrup. Pour water over the ham until the liquid is 5 cm (2 inches) from the rim of the cooker.
3 Cover and cook on low for 10 hours or until the ham is fork-tender. If possible, turn the ham over halfway through cooking.
4 Remove the ham from the cooker and slice thinly or break into pieces. Keep the cooking juices (about 2.25 L/9 cups) to cook whole potatoes, if desired.

SOUFFLÉED OMELETTE

Preparation 15 MINUTES   *Cook* 2 HOURS   *Serves* 6

When it comes to the slow cooker, one usually thinks of dishes cooked for many hours at a low temperature. But you can get surprisingly good results for recipes like souffléed omelette. Since there is never any room left in the oven when preparing a sugar shack meal, our slow cooker is the perfect solution for this delicious sugar shack treat.

60 mL (1/4 cup) all-purpose flour
5 mL (1 tsp) baking powder
2.5 mL (1/2 tsp) salt
10 eggs
375 mL (1-1/2 cups) milk
Pepper

1 Butter the inside of the slow cooker.
2 In a bowl, combine the flour, baking powder, and salt. Whisk in the eggs until smooth. Stir in the milk. Season with pepper.
3 Transfer to the cooker. Cover and cook on low for about 2 hours or until the omelette is nice and fluffy.
4 You can keep the souffléed omelette on warm for about an hour, covered. Serve as soon as you take the lid off. A soufflé collapses easily.

CREAM OF BUTTERNUT SQUASH SOUP WITH MAPLE SYRUP

Preparation 30 MINUTES   *Cook* 4 HOURS   *Serves* 4 TO 6   *Freezes well*

This soup showcases two of the most popular ingredients during maple syrup season: pork (bacon) and maple syrup. It adds a contemporary note to this time of the year.

Soup
1.5 L (6 cups) peeled and cubed butternut squash
875 mL (3-1/2 cups) chicken broth
60 mL (1/4 cup) maple syrup
1 onion, chopped
A pinch ground nutmeg
A pinch ground ginger
Salt and pepper

Bacon croutons
2 slices bacon, diced
30 mL (2 tbsp) olive oil
2 slices white bread, cut into small cubes

1 SOUP In the slow cooker, combine all the ingredients. Season with salt and pepper. Cover and cook on low for 4 hours. In a blender, purée the soup, using most but not all of the cooking liquid. Add more liquid if needed. Adjust the seasoning.

2 BACON CROUTONS In a skillet, brown the bacon in the oil. Add the bread cubes and brown them, stirring constantly. Serve the soup in bowls and garnish with the bacon croutons.

MAPLE-BRAISED PORK WITH PARSNIPS AND POTATOES

Preparation 20 MINUTES   *Cook* 9 HOURS   *Serves* 6

This is a recipe for beginners. You place everything in the slow cooker for 9 hours. It's as simple as that! The lemon juice adds a wonderful flavour, but it is also important for the parsnips—it prevents them from darkening.

500 mL (2 cups) apple cider
180 mL (3/4 cup) maple syrup
30 mL (2 tbsp) dry mustard
3 onions, thinly sliced
2 bay leaves
1 bone-in pork shoulder roast (about 1.4 kg/3 lb), not tied
454 g (1 lb) parsnips, peeled and halved lengthwise
12 baby red potatoes
30 mL (2 tbsp) olive oil
15 mL (1 tbsp) lemon juice
Salt and pepper

1 In the slow cooker, combine the cider, maple syrup, and dry mustard. Add the onions and bay leaves. Add the pork, making sure it is nestled well in the onions. Season with salt and pepper.

2 In a bowl, combine the parsnips and potatoes with the oil and lemon juice. Season with salt and pepper. Place the vegetables over the meat.

3 Cover and cook on low for 9 hours. The meat should be fork-tender.

poor man's maple pudding cake

RECIPE P156

WARM MAXIMUM 1 HOUR

POOR MAN'S MAPLE PUDDING CAKE

Preparation 20 MINUTES   *Cook* 2 HOURS   *Rest* 15 MINUTES   *Serves* 8

A sugar shack meal is not complete without a maple syrup dessert. Pudding cakes are easy to make in a slow cooker. Actually, the best slow cooker dessert recipes are the ones that require a lot of moisture. Another advantage when making these pudding cakes in the slow cooker: the sauce never spills over the sides or sticks to the bottom of the oven.

560 mL (2-1/4 cups) maple syrup (1 can)
500 mL (2 cups) 35% cream
500 mL (2 cups) all-purpose flour
5 mL (1 tsp) baking powder
1 mL (1/4 tsp) baking soda
1 mL (1/4 tsp) salt
125 mL (1/2 cup) unsalted butter, softened
180 mL (3/4 cup) sugar
2.5 mL (1/2 tsp) vanilla extract
2 eggs
180 mL (3/4 cup) milk

1 In a saucepan, bring the maple syrup and cream to a boil. Pour into the slow cooker.
2 In a bowl, combine the flour, baking powder, baking soda, and salt.
3 In another bowl, cream the butter, sugar, and vanilla with an electric mixer. Add the eggs, one at a time, beating until smooth after each addition. On low speed, add the dry ingredients, alternating with the milk. With an ice cream scoop or a large serving spoon, scoop the batter onto the hot syrup.
4 Place a clean cloth over the cooker, making sure it does not touch the batter, and cover with the lid. The cloth ensures that no water will drip onto the cake. Cook on high for 2 hours. Remove the lid and cloth and let rest for 15 minutes. Serve warm or cold.

the vegetarian *slow cooker*

Yes, absolutely, you read that right: veggies in the slow cooker! You are probably thinking, "What next, Ricardo? Will you be telling us that the slow cooker is ideal for drying clothes?" I might be exaggerating just a bit. So far, meat reigned supreme in the slow cooker. But there is room for plenty of other produce, like vegetables, tofu, and legumes. I know that for some, the words "vegetarian" and "flavourful" are just not compatible. If you add "slow cooker" to the mix, it is downright confusing. Well, I say go out on a limb and discover, or rediscover, some wonderful vegetarian dishes cooked in the slow cooker. And if, along with your vegetarian tendencies, you espouse ecological tendencies as well, then know that with a slow cooker you are consuming only about as much energy as a 100-watt light bulb.

recipes for vegetarians and not-so-vegetarians

WARM
MAXIMUM
2 HOURS

JAMAICAN-STYLE RED BEANS

Preparation 30 MINUTES   *Cook* 4 HOURS   *Serves* 4

Red beans, sweet potatoes, and coconut milk are well known at our table. Combining these three ingredients makes for a flavourful dish. For this recipe, we use canned red beans because sweet potatoes cook fairly quickly, and if we overcook them, they tend to fall apart.

1 can (398 mL/14 oz) coconut milk
5 mL (1 tsp) cornstarch
1 onion, finely chopped
30 mL (2 tbsp) olive oil
1 jalapeño pepper, seeded (or not), finely chopped
4 cloves garlic, finely chopped
500 mL (2 cups) peeled and cubed sweet potatoes
2 carrots, peeled and thinly sliced
1 can (540 mL/19 oz) red beans, rinsed and drained
1 can (398 mL/14 oz) diced tomatoes
1 red bell pepper, seeded and diced
10 mL (2 tsp) Cajun spices
5 mL (1 tsp) finely chopped peeled fresh ginger
125 mL (1/2 cup) finely chopped fresh cilantro
Salt and pepper

1 In the slow cooker, whisk together the coconut milk and cornstarch.
2 In a skillet, brown the onion in the oil. Add the jalapeño and garlic and cook for 1 minute. Transfer to the cooker. Add the remaining ingredients, except for the cilantro. Season with salt and pepper.
3 Cover and cook on low for 4 hours. Adjust the seasoning.
4 Serve on a bed of rice and sprinkle with the cilantro.

VEGETABLE SOUP

Preparation 20 MINUTES   *Cook* 8 HOURS   *Serves* 6 TO 8   *Freezes well*

In the fast-paced world we live in, homemade soup seems like a luxury—there just isn't enough time to make it. Slow cooker to the rescue! Thanks to this handy appliance, we can come home after a long day to a bowl of hearty, easy-to-prepare homemade soup. And all the great vitamins and flavours are richly concentrated.

1.5 L (6 cups) cubed green cabbage
1.5 L (6 cups) vegetable broth
1 can (796 mL/28 oz) diced tomatoes
4 carrots, peeled and diced
4 stalks celery, diced
6 green onions, thinly sliced
2 cloves garlic, finely chopped
2.5 mL (1/2 tsp) celery salt
Salt and pepper

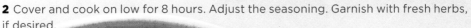

1 In the slow cooker, combine all the ingredients. Season with salt and pepper.
2 Cover and cook on low for 8 hours. Adjust the seasoning. Garnish with fresh herbs, if desired.

RECIPE P166

lentil stew with
poached eggs

LENTIL STEW WITH POACHED EGGS

Preparation 20 MINUTES   *Cook* 4 H 20   *Serves* 4

Finding different ways to eat legumes is sometimes a challenge. Here's a delicious one. Also perfect for brunch.

250 mL (1 cup) dried green lentils, rinsed and drained
500 mL (2 cups) vegetable broth
1 can (398 mL/14 oz) diced or crushed tomatoes
1 yellow bell pepper, seeded and diced
4 green onions, thinly sliced
1 jalapeño pepper, seeded and finely chopped
1 clove garlic, finely chopped
15 mL (1 tbsp) paprika
4 eggs
750 mL (3 cups) baby arugula
Salt and pepper

1 In the slow cooker, combine the lentils with the broth, tomatoes, bell pepper, green onions, jalapeño, garlic, and paprika. Season with salt and pepper.
2 Cover and cook on low for 4 hours. Adjust the seasoning.
3 If the stew has been kept on warm, bring the slow cooker up to high before breaking the eggs into the lentils. With a spoon or a ladle, make 4 holes in the lentil mixture. Break an egg into each hole. Season with salt and pepper. Cover and cook for 15 to 20 minutes more or until the egg whites are set. Serve with the arugula.

TOFU AND VEGETABLE CURRY

Preparation 30 MINUTES   *Cook* 4 HOURS   *Serves* 4

Meat has always been the preferred ingredient for the slow cooker. But we will show you that's not always the case. Tofu is a chameleon ingredient: it takes on the flavours of the other ingredients it's cooked with. Because slow cooking is just that—slow—the tofu has plenty of time to absorb all the wonderful flavours.

500 mL (2 cups) vegetable broth
30 mL (2 tbsp) cornstarch
15 mL (1 tbsp) curry powder
5 mL (1 tsp) ground cumin
5 mL (1 tsp) ground coriander
5 mL (1 tsp) ground turmeric
454 g (1 lb) firm tofu, diced
30 mL (2 tbsp) olive oil
3 cloves garlic, finely chopped
1 jalapeño pepper, seeded and finely chopped
1 red bell pepper, seeded and diced
1 L (4 cups) small cauliflower florets
1 can (398 mL/14 oz) chickpeas, rinsed and drained
60 mL (1/4 cup) currants
15 mL (1 tbsp) finely chopped peeled fresh ginger
5 mL (1 tsp) sambal oelek
Salt and pepper

1 In the slow cooker, combine the broth and half the cornstarch.
2 In a large bowl, combine the remaining cornstarch with the spices. Add the tofu and toss well, making sure the tofu is thoroughly coated.
3 In a large skillet, brown the tofu in the oil. Season with salt and pepper. Add the garlic and jalapeño and cook for 1 minute. Transfer to the cooker and add the remaining ingredients. Mix thoroughly.
4 Cover and cook on low for 4 hours. Adjust the seasoning.
5 Serve with rice or rice vermicelli.

RECIPE P167

tofu and vegetable curry

BLACK BEAN QUESADILLAS

Preparation 20 MINUTES   *Cook* 8 HOURS   *Serves* 4

Unlike most beans, black beans do not need to be soaked before slow cooking. They cook while you are at work or busy doing other things. When you get home, all that is left to do is brown the quesadillas in a skillet. No time for browning? Use the black beans as a filling for tacos with chopped lettuce, salsa, sour cream, and grated cheese.

Black bean filling
250 mL (1 cup) dried black beans, rinsed and drained
375 mL (1-1/2 cups) vegetable broth
375 mL (1-1/2 cups) store-bought salsa
375 mL (1-1/2 cups) fresh or frozen corn kernels
125 mL (1/2 cup) finely chopped fresh cilantro
Salt and pepper

Quesadillas
8 large tortillas
1 L (4 cups) grated mozzarella cheese
30 mL (2 tbsp) olive oil
Sour cream
Store-bought salsa

1 BLACK BEANS In the slow cooker, combine the black beans, broth, and salsa. Season with salt and pepper.

2 Cover and cook on low for 8 hours (or 10 hours if you like very tender beans). You can keep the black beans on warm. Add the corn, cover, and cook on low for 5 to 10 minutes more (depending on whether the corn is fresh or frozen), until the corn is cooked. If you have kept the beans on warm for more than 1 hour, bring it up to high before adding the corn.

3 Drain the black beans if there is too much liquid (depending on the type of slow cooker). Adjust the seasoning.

4 QUESADILLAS Arrange the tortillas on a flat surface. Sprinkle 45 mL (3 tbsp) of the cheese on half of each tortilla. Add 125 mL (1/2 cup) of the black bean filling per tortilla and then another 45 mL (3 tbsp) of cheese. Fold the tortillas in half. Press gently.

5 In 2 large non-stick skillets over low heat, brown 4 quesadillas at a time in the oil, about 3 minutes per side. Cut into wedges and top with sour cream and salsa.

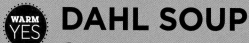

DAHL SOUP

Preparation 20 MINUTES   **Cook** 6 HOURS   *Serves* 6 TO 8   *Freezes well*

Why does this soup use both green and red lentils? One of them falls apart during cooking and the other remains whole and tender—a perfect mix of textures. Make sure you brown the onions and the spices before placing them in the slow cooker. This step is crucial to enjoying 100% more flavour.

3 onions, finely chopped
45 mL (3 tbsp) butter
5 mL (1 tsp) ground turmeric
5 mL (1 tsp) ground cumin
5 mL (1 tsp) ground coriander
5 mL (1 tsp) chili powder
1 mL (1/4 tsp) ground cardamom
1 mL (1/4 tsp) cayenne pepper
3 cloves garlic, finely chopped
1.75 L (7 cups) vegetable broth
250 mL (1 cup) dried red lentils, rinsed and drained
250 mL (1 cup) dried green lentils, rinsed and drained
One 2.5 cm (1-inch) piece fresh ginger, peeled
125 mL (1/2 cup) plain 10% yogurt
125 mL (1/2 cup) finely chopped fresh cilantro
Lime wedges
Salt and pepper

1 In a large skillet, lightly brown the onions in the butter. Season with salt and pepper. Add the spices and garlic and cook for 1 minute, stirring constantly. Deglaze with 125 mL (1/2 cup) of the vegetable broth, scraping the bottom of the skillet to get at all the spices. Transfer to the slow cooker and add the remaining broth, the lentils, and ginger. Season with salt and pepper.
2 Cover and cook on low for 6 hours. Remove the ginger and adjust the seasoning. Add broth or water if needed.
3 Serve in bowls. Garnish with the yogurt and sprinkle with the cilantro. Serve with a lime wedge. Delicious with naan bread.

RECIPE P177

vegetable and chickpea couscous

VEGETABLE AND CHICKPEA COUSCOUS

Preparation 30 MINUTES   *Cook* 5 HOURS   *Serves* 6

Couscous in a slow cooker? The idea is to cook the vegetables and the chickpeas in a good broth for part of the day. When you are just about ready to serve, ladle some of the hot cooking juices from the slow cooker into the couscous and let it rest for 5 minutes to absorb the liquid.

Vegetable stew
2 onions, chopped
30 mL (2 tbsp) olive oil
2 cloves garlic, chopped
5 mL (1 tsp) ground turmeric
5 mL (1 tsp) ground cumin
750 mL (3 cups) water
1 can (398 mL/14 oz) diced tomatoes
1 can (398 mL/14 oz) chickpeas, rinsed and drained
5 carrots, peeled and sliced
2 white turnips, peeled, each cut into 6 wedges
2 different-coloured bell peppers, seeded and cubed
1 small rutabaga, peeled and cubed
2 zucchinis, cut into half-slices
15 mL (1 tbsp) honey
15 mL (1 tbsp) harissa
60 mL (1/4 cup) finely chopped fresh cilantro
Salt and pepper

Couscous
625 mL (2-1/2 cups) medium couscous
15 mL (1 tbsp) olive oil

1 VEGETABLE STEW In a large skillet, brown the onions in the oil. Add the garlic and spices and cook for 1 minute. Transfer to the slow cooker. Add the remaining ingredients, except for the cilantro. Mix thoroughly. Season with salt and pepper. Cover and cook on high for 5 hours.

2 COUSCOUS Ladle 625 mL (2-1/2 cups) of the hot cooking liquid from the slow cooker into a bowl. (If the vegetables have been kept on warm, heat the cooking liquid in the microwave oven, or the liquid will not be hot enough to cook the couscous.) Add the couscous and the oil, and stir. Cover and let rest for 5 minutes. Fluff the couscous with a fork.

3 When ready to serve the stew, stir in the cilantro. Serve the couscous with the vegetable stew.

SUN-DRIED TOMATO AND OLIVE STRATA

Preparation 30 MINUTES   *Soak* 2 HOURS   *Cook* 3 HOURS   *Serves* 4 TO 6

If you like frittatas, you will love this Italian version of savoury bread pudding. I would have liked to add grated cheese to the recipe, but unfortunately slow cooking can curdle milk, and cheese becomes oily. The few exceptions are evaporated milk, dry cheeses like Parmesan, and processed cheese.

6 eggs, lightly beaten
1 can (370 mL/13 oz) evaporated milk
125 mL (1/2 cup) 35% cream
1.5 L (6 cups) cubed stale bread
125 mL (1/2 cup) oil-packed sun-dried tomatoes, drained and chopped
125 mL (1/2 cup) finely chopped fresh chives
125 mL (1/2 cup) grated Parmigiano-Reggiano cheese
60 mL (1/4 cup) oil-packed dried black olives, drained, pitted, and chopped
Salt and pepper

1 In a bowl, whisk together the eggs, evaporated milk, and cream. Add the remaining ingredients. Season with salt and pepper. Mix thoroughly. Let soak for 2 hours at room temperature or in the refrigerator overnight.
2 Butter the inside of the slow cooker. Pour in the egg mixture. Cover and cook on low for 3 hours. Serve with a green salad.

VEGETARIAN SPAGHETTI SAUCE

Preparation 40 MINUTES **_Cook_** 8 HOURS **_Quantity_** 3 L (12 CUPS)
Freezes well

When "meatless ground round" is one of the ingredients in a recipe, it doesn't always end up being a hit. It is, however, a great source of protein and gives this sauce a wonderful texture. Meatless ground round is a soy-based product that looks like cooked ground meat and can be found in the produce section of your grocery store. Of course, you can use real ground meat if you like, and brown it along with the onions.

2 onions, finely chopped
225 g (8 oz) white button or other mushrooms, finely chopped
45 mL (3 tbsp) olive oil
340 g (3/4 lb) meatless ground round
30 mL (2 tbsp) tomato paste
4 cloves garlic, finely chopped
250 mL (1 cup) white wine
1 can (796 mL/28 oz) diced tomatoes
750 mL (3 cups) homemade or store-bought tomato sauce
4 carrots, peeled and finely chopped
4 stalks celery, finely chopped
2.5 mL (1/2 tsp) dried oregano
2 bay leaves
Salt and pepper

1 In a large skillet, brown the onions and mushrooms in the oil. Season with salt and pepper. Add the meatless ground round, tomato paste, and garlic and cook for 1 minute, stirring constantly. Deglaze with the white wine. Transfer to the slow cooker. Add the remaining ingredients. Mix thoroughly. Season with salt and pepper.
2 Cover and cook on low for 8 hours. Remove the bay leaves. Adjust the seasoning.

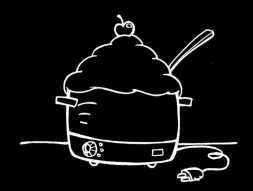

the slow cooker
for desserts

When you're entertaining guests and it's time for dessert, sometimes there are just no topics of conversation left. Instead of having a lull at the table, imagine telling your guests that you have made cheesecake in the slow cooker! Either the conversation goes on for another twenty minutes or your guests leave rather quickly. Either way, you're covered! You no longer need to worry about a temperamental oven or how high the rack should sit. You don't have to watch over your pudding or the rising of your cheesecake. The slow cooker is your best bet for perfect results. Your dessert smells wonderful, nothing burns, and the oven is free to cook your main dish.

recipes for a sweet ending

BROWNIES

Preparation 15 MINUTES   ***Cook*** 2 H 15   ***Cool*** 1 HOUR
Serves 8   ***Freezes well***

**When preparing desserts in a slow cooker, you might need to make
some adjustments the first time you try them. Depending on how
powerful your appliance is, the outer edge of your brownies may be
over- or underdone. The more you use your slow cooker, the better you
will get to know it, and the better the results.**

140 g (5 oz) dark chocolate, chopped
180 mL (3/4 cup) unsalted butter, cubed
250 mL (1 cup) sugar
2 eggs
5 mL (1 tsp) vanilla extract
1 mL (1/4 tsp) salt
125 mL (1/2 cup) all-purpose flour
180 mL (3/4 cup) walnuts or pecans, toasted and chopped (optional)

1 Butter the inside of the slow cooker. Place a large strip of parchment paper in the
bottom, letting it extend up the sides.
2 In a bowl over a double boiler or in the microwave oven, melt the chocolate with
the butter. Remove the bowl from the double boiler and let it cool. Whisk in the
sugar. Whisk in the eggs, vanilla, and salt. Add the flour and stir for about 2 minutes.
Stir in the nuts, if using. Transfer to the cooker.
3 Cover and cook on low for about 2 hours and 15 minutes. The cooking time may
vary from one slow cooker to another. The edges of the brownies must be thoroughly
cooked while the centre should be softer. Remove the inside container from the slow
cooker. Let cool for 1 hour with the lid on. Remove the lid. Serve warm or let cool
completely. Run a thin blade around the brownie and unmould.

RECIPE P186

brownies

RICE PUDDING

Preparation 10 MINUTES   **Cook** 3 HOURS   **Refrigerate** 4 HOURS
Serves 6

When I was a youngster, my mother made this recipe with milk, parboiled rice, and raisins. She stirred it a very long time. No more stirring with a slow cooker. We use short-grain rice and add cream for a more festive pudding. Beware, however, as evaporation and temperature may vary among models of slow cookers. If the cold pudding is too thick, just add some milk.

1/2 vanilla bean (or 5 mL/1 tsp vanilla extract)
930 mL (3-3/4 cups) milk
180 mL (3/4 cup) arborio rice
250 mL (1 cup) 35% cream
180 mL (3/4 cup) sugar

1 Split the vanilla bean in half lengthwise. With the tip of a sharp knife, scrape out the seeds and place them in the slow cooker along with the pod. If you are using vanilla extract, add it only at the very end.
2 Add the milk, rice, 125 mL (1/2 cup) of the cream, and the sugar.
3 Cover and cook on low for about 3 hours or until the rice is tender. Stir in the vanilla extract, if using. Transfer to a sealable container and refrigerate for 4 hours or overnight. Remove the vanilla pod.
4 In a bowl, whip the remaining cream until firm. With a spatula, gently fold the cream into the rice mixture. If it is still too thick, add a little milk.

CHEESECAKE

Preparation 30 MINUTES   *Cook* 1 H 30   *Refrigerate* 4 HOURS
Serves 4   *Cheesecake freezes well*

Cheesecake is something we don't make often because with a yield of twelve pieces, we seem to be eating it for two weeks! Not only does the slow cooker guarantee a perfect texture to the cake (because the process is very much like a double boiler, which prevents the cake from cracking), but we use ramekins, which yield four portions. When ready to serve, we add a graham cracker crumble and diced strawberries to make it taste like traditional cheesecake.

Cheesecake
1 package (250 g/8 oz) cream cheese, softened
75 mL (1/3 cup) sugar
1 egg
60 mL (1/4 cup) 35% cream
5 mL (1 tsp) vanilla extract

Crumble
125 mL (1/2 cup) graham cracker crumbs
60 mL (1/4 cup) all-purpose flour
30 mL (2 tbsp) brown sugar
60 mL (1/4 cup) unsalted butter, softened

Strawberries
250 mL (1 cup) fresh strawberries, diced
15 mL (1 tbsp) sugar

1 CHEESECAKE Place a clean cloth in the bottom of the slow cooker to prevent the ramekins from shifting.

2 In a food processor, purée all the ingredients until smooth. Pour into four 125 mL (1/2-cup) ramekins. Place the ramekins in the cooker and carefully pour in enough hot water to come halfway up the sides of the ramekins.

3 Cover and cook on low from 1 hour and 15 minutes to 1 hour and 30 minutes or until firm and slightly puffed up. Remove the ramekins from the slow cooker and let cool. Cover with plastic wrap. Refrigerate for at least 4 hours or until completely chilled.

4 CRUMBLE With the rack in the middle position, preheat the oven to 180°C (350°F). Line a baking sheet with parchment paper.

5 In a bowl, combine the dry ingredients. Add the butter and mix until crumbly. With your fingers, drop the crumble in small pieces on the baking sheet. Bake, stirring twice during cooking, for about 15 minutes or until golden brown. Let cool.

6 STRAWBERRIES Toss the strawberries with the sugar. Set aside for 5 minutes to macerate.

7 When ready to serve, garnish each ramekin with graham cracker crumble and strawberries.

LEMON PUDDING CAKE

Preparation 20 MINUTES   ***Cook*** 3 HOURS   ***Rest*** 30 MINUTES   ***Serves*** 8

Lemon and caramel are my two favourite dessert flavours. Lemon in the summer and caramel in the winter.

Lemon curd
375 mL (1-1/2 cups) sugar
20 mL (4 tsp) cornstarch
2 eggs
60 mL (1/4 cup) unsalted butter, melted
375 mL (1-1/2 cups) water
180 mL (3/4 cup) lemon juice

Batter
375 mL (1-1/2 cups) all-purpose flour
10 mL (2 tsp) baking powder
A pinch salt
125 mL (1/2 cup) sugar
125 mL (1/2 cup) canola oil
1 lemon, grated zest only
2 eggs
125 mL (1/2 cup) milk

1 LEMON CURD In the slow cooker, combine the sugar and cornstarch. Whisk in the eggs and melted butter. Add the water and lemon juice and whisk until smooth.

2 BATTER In a bowl, combine the flour, baking powder, and salt.

3 In another bowl, beat the sugar, oil, and lemon zest with an electric mixer. Add the eggs, one at a time, and beat until smooth. On low speed, add the dry ingredients, alternating with the milk. With an ice cream scoop or a large spoon, scoop 8 balls of batter onto the curd.

4 Place a clean cloth over the slow cooker, making sure it does not touch the batter, and cover with the lid. The cloth ensures that no water will drip onto the cake. Cook on high for 3 hours. Remove the lid and cloth and let rest for 30 minutes. Serve warm or cold.

cheesecake

chocolate pudding
cake

RECIPE P199

CHOCOLATE PUDDING CAKE

Preparation 30 MINUTES   *Cook* 2 HOURS   *Rest* 15 MINUTES   *Serves* 8

Decadent! My oven always seems busy with the main dish when I entertain guests. So the slow cooker comes to my rescue for this pudding cake that I like to serve warm.

Sauce
560 mL (2-1/4 cups) brown sugar
125 mL (1/2 cup) cocoa powder, sifted
15 mL (1 tbsp) cornstarch
115 g (4 oz) dark chocolate, coarsely chopped
375 mL (1-1/2 cups) water
375 mL (1-1/2 cups) 35% or half-and-half cream
2.5 mL (1/2 tsp) vanilla extract

Cake
375 mL (1-1/2 cups) all-purpose flour
2.5 mL (1/2 tsp) baking powder
2.5 mL (1/2 tsp) baking soda
A pinch salt
180 mL (3/4 cup) unsalted butter, softened
250 mL (1 cup) sugar
75 mL (1/3 cup) cocoa powder, sifted
1 egg
1 egg yolk
180 mL (3/4 cup) milk

1 SAUCE In a saucepan, combine the brown sugar, cocoa powder, and cornstarch. Add the remaining ingredients. Bring to a boil while whisking, then simmer for 10 seconds. Transfer to the slow cooker.
2 CAKE In a bowl, combine the flour, baking powder, baking soda, and salt.
3 In another bowl, cream the butter, sugar, and cocoa powder with an electric mixer. Add the egg and egg yolk and beat until smooth. On low speed, add the dry ingredients, alternating with the milk. With an ice cream scoop or a large spoon, scoop the batter onto the hot chocolate sauce.
4 Place a clean cloth over the slow cooker, making sure it does not touch the batter, and cover with the lid. The cloth ensures that no water will drip onto the cake.
5 Cook on high for 2 hours. Remove the inside container from the slow cooker. Remove the lid and cloth and let rest for 15 minutes. Serve warm or cold. Reheat if needed.

RECIPE P203

crème brûlée

CRÈME BRÛLÉE

Preparation 10 MINUTES　　　*Cook* 2 HOURS　　　*Refrigerate* 4 HOURS
Serves 4

Not all desserts are a success in the slow cooker. But those that need cooking in a water bath are excellent candidates. Cheesecake, crème caramel, and crème brûlée are ideal for the slow cooker.

4 egg yolks
75 mL (1/3 cup) sugar
1/2 vanilla bean, seeds only, or 2.5 mL (1/2 tsp) vanilla extract
375 mL (1-1/2 cups) 35% cream
Sugar for caramelizing

1 In the bottom of the slow cooker, place a clean cloth to prevent the ramekins from shifting.
2 In a bowl, combine the egg yolks, sugar, and vanilla seeds. Whisk until well blended. Add the cream and mix thoroughly.
3 Pour into four 125 mL (1/2-cup) ramekins. Place the ramekins in the cooker and carefully pour in enough hot water to come halfway up the sides of the ramekins.
4 Cover and cook on low for 2 hours or until the custard has set. The centre should still jiggle. Remove the ramekins from the cooker and let cool. Cover with plastic wrap. Refrigerate for at least 4 hours or until completely chilled.
5 When ready to serve, sprinkle a thin layer of sugar on top and caramelize with a culinary torch. Serve immediately.

BREAD PUDDING WITH RUM SAUCE

Preparation 30 MINUTES   ***Cook*** 2 H 30   ***Refrigerate*** 2 HOURS
Serves 6 TO 8

With rum sauce, even a simple and inexpensive dessert like bread pudding can become a gourmet experience.

Bread pudding
4 eggs
180 mL (3/4 cup) brown sugar
1 mL (1/4 tsp) cinnamon (optional)
1 can (370 mL/13 oz) evaporated milk
250 mL (1 cup) 35% cream
1.5 L (6 cups) tightly packed cubed stale egg bread
30 mL (2 tbsp) currants (optional)
45 mL (3 tbsp) sliced almonds, toasted

Rum sauce
60 mL (1/4 cup) sugar
5 mL (1 tsp) cornstarch
4 egg yolks
375 mL (1-1/2 cups) 15% or half-and-half cream
15 mL (1 tbsp) dark rum

1 BREAD PUDDING Generously butter the inside of the slow cooker.
2 In the cooker, combine the eggs, 125 mL (1/2 cup) of the brown sugar, and cinnamon, if using. Stir in the evaporated milk and cream. Add the bread and the currants, if using. Mix thoroughly. Sprinkle with the almonds and the remaining brown sugar.
3 Place a clean cloth over the cooker, making sure it does not touch the pudding, and cover with the lid. The cloth ensures that no water will drip onto the pudding. Cook on low for 2 hours and 30 minutes. Remove the lid and cloth and let cool for 15 minutes.
4 RUM SAUCE Meanwhile, in a small saucepan, combine the sugar and cornstarch off the heat. Add the egg yolks and whisk until smooth. Stir in the cream and rum.
5 Cook over medium-low heat, stirring constantly with a wooden spoon or a spatula, until the sauce thickens and coats the back of a spoon. Strain into a bowl. Place plastic wrap directly on the surface of the sauce. Let cool. Refrigerate for 2 hours or until completely chilled. Serve the pudding, warm or cold, with the sauce.

APPLE AND NUT CAKE

Preparation 30 MINUTES   *Cook* 3 HOURS   *Rest* 15 MINUTES   *Serves* 8 TO 10

Pudding-cake desserts are usually cooked on high. The low setting is not hot enough for the cake to rise properly.

Apple filling
180 mL (3/4 cup) brown sugar
15 mL (1 tbsp) all-purpose flour
6 Cortland apples, peeled and thinly sliced
60 mL (1/4 cup) unsalted butter, melted
60 mL (1/4 cup) 35% cream or apple juice

Cake
375 mL (1-1/2 cups) all-purpose flour
10 mL (2 tsp) baking powder
1 mL (1/4 tsp) salt
125 mL (1/2 cup) unsalted butter, softened
180 mL (3/4 cup) brown sugar
2.5 mL (1/2 tsp) vanilla extract
2 eggs
125 mL (1/2 cup) milk

Nut topping
30 mL (2 tbsp) unsalted butter
60 mL (1/4 cup) brown sugar
250 mL (1 cup) walnuts, coarsely chopped

1 APPLE FILLING Butter the inside of the slow cooker. Add the brown sugar and flour and stir. Add the remaining ingredients and combine thoroughly.

2 CAKE In a bowl, combine the flour, baking powder, and salt.

3 In another bowl, cream the butter, brown sugar, and vanilla with an electric mixer. Add the eggs, one at a time, and beat until smooth. On low speed, add the dry ingredients, alternating with the milk. Spread the batter over the apples.

4 NUT TOPPING In a saucepan or the microwave oven, melt the butter with the brown sugar. Add the walnuts and stir thoroughly. Spread over the batter.

5 Cover and cook on high for 3 hours. Remove the lid and let rest for 15 minutes. Serve warm or cold with vanilla ice cream.

STICKY TOFFEE PUDDING

Preparation 30 MINUTES   **Cook** 3 H 15   **Serves** 8

A dessert to die for. We place a cloth under the lid to absorb the extra steam. This way, the top of the cake will not get wet.

Caramel sauce
500 mL (2 cups) 35% cream
500 mL (2 cups) brown sugar
30 mL (2 tbsp) unsalted or semi-salted butter

Cake
180 mL (3/4 cup) water
250 mL (1 cup) pitted dates, finely chopped
5 mL (1 tsp) baking soda
500 mL (2 cups) all-purpose flour
125 mL (1/2 cup) unsalted or semi-salted butter, softened
125 mL (1/2 cup) sugar
5 mL (1 tsp) vanilla extract
2 eggs
180 mL (3/4 cup) milk

1 CARAMEL SAUCE In a saucepan, bring all the ingredients to a boil, stirring constantly. Reduce for about 5 minutes. Set aside.

2 CAKE In a saucepan, bring the water and dates to a boil. Add 1 mL (1/4 tsp) of the baking soda and mix thoroughly. Remove from the heat and let cool.

3 In a bowl, combine the flour and the remaining 4 mL (3/4 tsp) of baking soda.

4 In another bowl, cream the butter, sugar, and vanilla with an electric mixer. Add the eggs, one at a time, and beat until smooth. On low speed, add the dry ingredients, alternating with the milk. Stir in the date mixture.

5 Spread the batter in the slow cooker. Pour half the caramel sauce over the batter. Place a clean cloth over the slow cooker, making sure it does not touch the batter, and cover with the lid. Cook on low for 3 hours. With a skewer, pierce holes all over the surface of the cake and drizzle with the remaining caramel sauce. Continue cooking for 15 minutes, uncovered. Serve hot or warm.

MAPLE BAKED APPLES

Preparation 15 MINUTES   ***Cook*** 3 HOURS (high) OR 4 HOURS (low)   ***Serves*** 4

When I was a child, my mother used to make baked apples with maple syrup. This is the same dish, only made in the slow cooker. So the apples don't burst open, make a small incision all around the fruit before cooking them. This is an excellent weeknight dessert.

125 mL (1/2 cup) maple syrup
60 mL (1/4 cup) apple juice
4 Cortland or Gala apples
125 mL (1/2 cup) quick-cooking rolled oats
60 mL (1/4 cup) maple sugar or brown sugar
60 mL (1/4 cup) unsalted butter, softened
A pinch cinnamon

1 Pour the maple syrup and apple juice into the slow cooker.
2 With a sharp knife, make a small incision all around the middle of the apples so they don't burst while cooking. With a melon baller, remove the apple cores, forming a hole of about 45 mL (3 tbsp). Set the apples aside.
3 In a bowl, combine the oats, maple sugar, butter, and cinnamon. Fill each apple cavity with the oat mixture. Place in the slow cooker.
4 Cover and cook on high for 3 hours or on low for 4 hours. Make sure there is always enough liquid during cooking.
5 Serve the apples with the cooking juices and a scoop of vanilla ice cream.

CRÈME CARAMEL

Preparation 15 MINUTES   ***Cook*** 4 HOURS (low) OR 1 H 30 (high)
Refrigerate 4 HOURS   ***Serves*** 4

This great French classic is not necessarily as easy to prepare as it might seem when cooked in the traditional way. Bubbles in the custard mean the heat was too intense or it overcooked. The slow cooker keeps the temperature even and prevents overcooking. For a more decadent crème caramel, replace 125 mL (1/2 cup) of the milk with 35% cream.

Caramel
125 mL (1/2 cup) sugar
45 mL (3 tbsp) water

Custard
2 eggs
1 egg yolk
60 mL (1/4 cup) sugar
375 mL (1-1/2 cups) milk
5 mL (1 tsp) vanilla extract

1 CARAMEL In a small saucepan, bring the sugar and water to a boil. Cook, without stirring, until the caramel is golden brown. Divide among four 125 mL (1/2-cup) ramekins. Let cool.

2 CUSTARD Place a clean cloth in the bottom of the slow cooker to prevent the ramekins from shifting.

3 In a bowl, beat the eggs, egg yolk, and sugar until smooth. Stir in the milk and vanilla. Divide among the ramekins.

4 Place the ramekins in the slow cooker. Carefully add enough hot water to come halfway up the sides of the ramekins. Cover and cook on low for about 4 hours or on high for about 1 hour and 30 minutes, or until the custard is set. The middle should still jiggle.

5 Remove the ramekins from the slow cooker and let cool. Cover with plastic wrap and refrigerate for at least 4 hours or until completely chilled.

6 When ready to serve, slide a thin blade all around the ramekins and turn upside down onto a plate. Serve cold.

More about your
slow cooker

About legumes

Beans, peas, and other legumes are well suited to the slow cooker. During our tests, we tried skipping **the soaking step,** thinking that long, slow cooking on low heat would do the trick. Unfortunately, in a number of cases, the legumes were undercooked. There are three exceptions to the soaking requirement: lentils, split peas, and black beans. **All other legumes must be soaked before cooking, using either of these two methods:**

TRADITIONAL SOAKING
Place the legumes in a large bowl and cover them with water. Let them soak at room temperature for at least 6 to 8 hours; overnight is best. Add more water as needed. The legumes must always be covered with at least 2.5 cm (1 inch) of water. Drain and discard the soaking water.

QUICK SOAKING
Place the legumes in a large saucepan and cover them with cold water. Bring to a boil, then simmer for 2 minutes. Cover the pot, remove from the heat, and let sit for about 2 hours. Drain and discard the soaking water.

LEGUMES	SOAKING	COOKING
Lentils	no	4 hours
Split peas	no	6 hours
Black beans	no	8 hours (10 hours for very tender beans)
Red beans	yes	8 hours
Navy beans	yes	8 hours (10 hours for baked beans because of the sugar)
Chickpeas	yes	8 hours

5 things

YOU SHOULD KNOW BEFORE YOU BUY

After purchasing a number of different models to fine-tune the recipes in this book, I concluded that buying a good slow cooker is not an easy task. There are models at $39.99 as well as models at $400, but price is not always a true indicator of quality. I won't recommend any particular brand. It is best to consult the latest consumer's guide or friends who like their own particular slow cooker. However, I can give you my personal buying criteria.

1. Because this appliance will last almost a lifetime, keep in mind that it will serve many purposes, so going for a fair-sized slow cooker is best. A 6-quart (5.6 L) capacity is ideal. It is what I use. And we used this size to fine-tune the recipes in this book. You can cook a ham or a whole chicken in it.

2. An oval-shaped slow cooker is far more practical than a round one. A whole chicken, for example, is more difficult to place in a round container.

3. Make sure you can set the number of hours required, both on high and low settings.

4. Choose a slow cooker with a warm setting as well. Once the cooking time is done, the appliance will automatically set itself on warm. Some recipes cook for 4 hours, and the food should stay warm until you get home a couple of hours later.

5. Those little extras (thermometers, double settings) are not really useful and just boost the price. Choose a basic model that offers various settings.

Your own recipes in the slow cooker

To **adapt your regular recipes** to the slow cooker, whether it is your osso buco or your grandmother's stew, here are **a few simple rules**.

1. The recipe must call for simmering or braising with very little liquid.

2. You must reduce the amount of liquid called for by about half, since there is very little evaporation from the slow cooker. If you have used too much liquid and your stew looks like a soup, remove the solid pieces and cook the liquid on high. A quicker way is to transfer the broth to a saucepan and cook it down on the stove. Either way, reduce the broth until you get the consistency you want.

3. The slow cooker must always be either half full or two-thirds full, no more, no less. If there is more in the container, the appliance will take too long to heat the contents. If, on the other hand, there is too little in the container, you will have to check regularly to ensure the food does not overcook.

4. Find a recipe in my book that is similar to yours and use it as a guide for cooking time. Most meat and vegetable recipes need to be cooked on low for 6 to 8 hours.

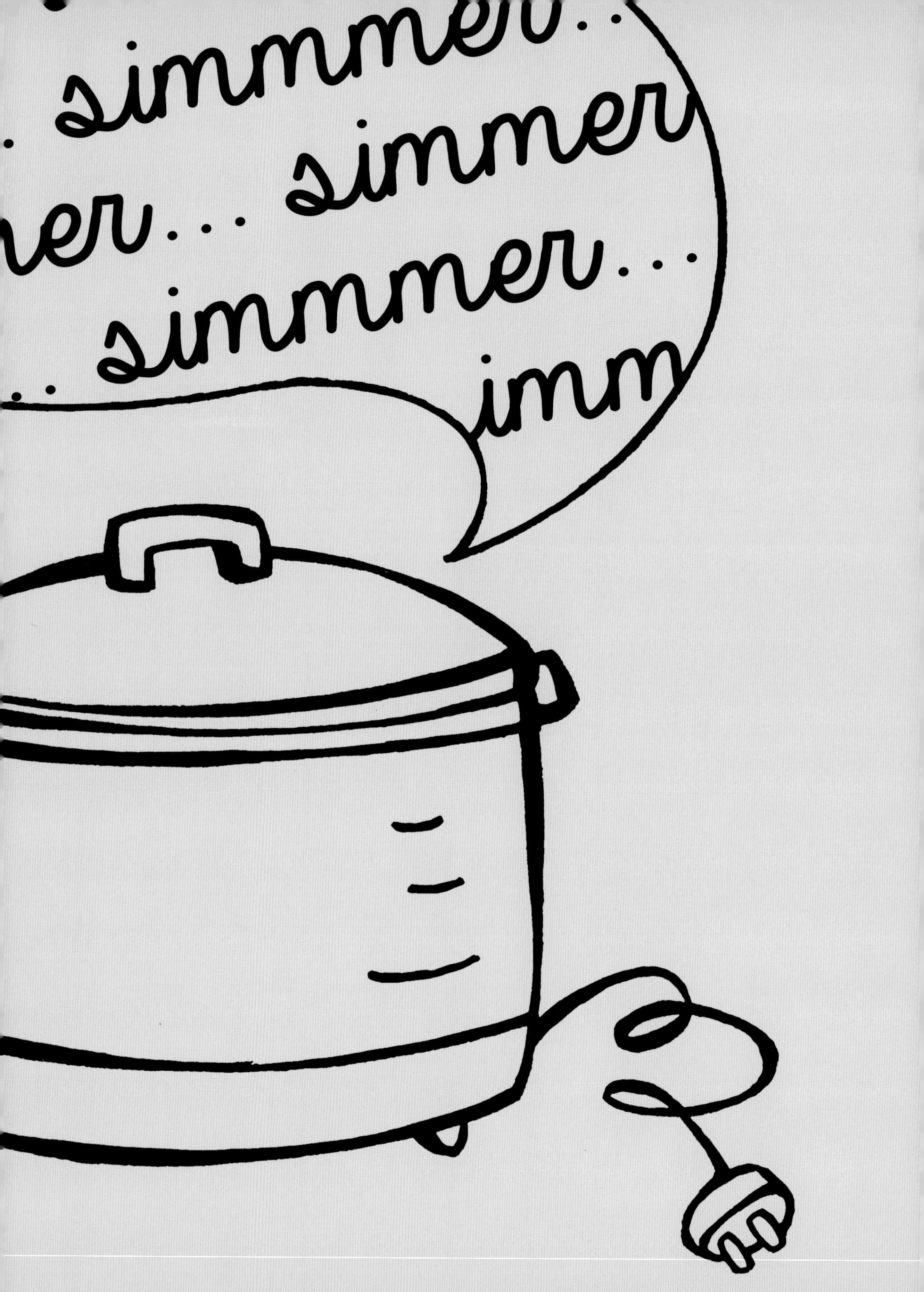

. simmmer. . .
ner. . . simmer
. . . simmmer. . .
imm

THANK YOU... THANK YOU... THANK YOU... THANK YOU...

Brigitte always knew there was a need for a book such as this. She knows how hard it is to run around trying to get everything done and have dinner with the family as well. The slow cooker is one way to be able to do just that: eat a homemade meal together. Thank you for all our family dinners.

A cookbook is the product of the efforts of a number of people. I have been working with the same wonderful team for years now. In the kitchen, thank you to Nataly, Étienne, Danielle, and lastly Kareen, who toiled and believed in this project from the very beginning.

The difference between a regular manuscript (written text on sheets of white paper) and a completed book is the work done by the creative team. Thank you to Sonia Bluteau, the team's intrepid leader. Your idea of hooking a slow cooker onto a maple tree had me in stitches. Your whimsy is always expressed with the best of taste. Thank you to my loyal friend of ten years, Christian Lacroix. Along with Anne and Sylvain, you gave the slow cooker quite a personality from behind your lens. Thank you, Geneviève—the design is a great success because of you. And Rodolphe, kudos for your illustrations. Each and every one of them made me laugh.

Thank you to Caroline Jamet and Martine Pelletier from Les Editions La Presse for your patience and your unwavering confidence.

Thank you to all my tasters, both at home and at work.

And thank you to you, dear readers. I remain grounded because of you, and I always remember that the most important ingredient in any recipe is the people with whom we share it.

...oth +++ Chicken cacciatore +++ Chocolate pudding cake +++ Coq...
...n +++ Cream of butternut squash soup with maple syrup +++ Crè...
...rûlée +++ Crème caramel +++ Dahl soup +++ Date and lemon chick...
...jine +++ Flemish carbonnade +++ Garden ratatouille +++ Goulash +...
...oney chicken wings +++ Jamaican-style red beans +++ Lamb nava...
...+ Lamb shanks with prunes +++ Lasagna +++ Layered "stuffe...
...abbage +++ Lemon pudding cake +++ Lentil stew with poached eg...
...+ Lime bavette rolls +++ Mango "jam" +++ Maple baked apples +...
...aple and beer-braised ham +++ Maple-braised pork with parsni...
...nd potatoes +++ Meatloaf +++ Orange and honey turkey breast +...
...range-braised beet salad +++ Osso buco +++ Pea soup +++ Pineapp...
...hicken +++ Poor man's maple pudding cake +++ Pork chili +++ Pull...
...ork burgers +++ Rabbit braised in red wine with pancetta +++ Ri...
...+ Rice pudding +++ Rouille +++ Salsa verde pork tacos +++ Salt po...
...+ Scalloped potatoes +++ Seafood and fish soup with fresh herbs...
...ouffléed omelette +++ Steamed salmon with fennel +++ Sticky toff...
...udding +++ Strawberry "jam" +++ Strawberry and rhubarb "jam"...
...n-dried tomato and olive strata +++ Tofu and vegetable curry +...
...eal cheeks with figs +++ Vegetable and chickpea couscous +...
...egetable soup +++ Vegetarian spaghetti sauce +++ Whole chicken +...
...pple and nut cake +++ Baked beans +++ Barbecued pulled pork +...
...ef and carrot stew +++ Beef and chickpea soup +++ Beef strogan...
...+ Beef teriyaki +++ Black bean quesadillas +++ Blue cheese dip +...
...olognese sauce +++ Braised carrots +++ Bread pudding with ru...
...auce +++ Brownies +++ Cheesecake + Chicken broth +++ Chick...
...acciatore +++ Chocolate pudding cake +++ Coq au vin +++ Crea...
... butternut squash soup with maple syrup +++ Crème brûlée +++...
...rème caramel +++ Dahl soup +++ Date and lemon chicken tajine +...
...emish carbonnade +++ Garden ratatouille +++ Goulash +++ Hon...
...hicken wings +++ Jamaican-style red beans +++ Lamb navarin +...
...amb shanks with prunes +++ Lasagna +++ Layered "stuffed" cabba...
...+ Lemon pudding cake +++ Lentil stew with poached eggs +...
...me bavette rolls +++ Mango "jam" +++ Maple baked apples +...
...aple and beer-braised ham +++ Maple-braised pork with parsni...
...nd potatoes +++ Meatloaf +++ Orange and honey turkey breast +...
...range-braised beet salad +++ Osso buco +++ Pea soup +++ Pineapp...
...hicken +++ Poor man's maple pudding cake +++ Pork chili +++ Pull...
...ork burgers +++ Rabbit braised in red wine with pancetta +++ Ri...
...+ Rice pudding +++ Rouille +++ Salsa verde pork tacos +++ Salt po...
...+ Scalloped potatoes +++ Seafood and fish soup with fresh herbs +...
...ouffléed omelette +++ Steamed salmon with fennel +++ Sticky toff...
...udding +++ Strawberry "jam" +++ Strawberry and rhubarb "jam"+...
...n-dried tomato and olive strata +++ Tofu and vegetable curry +...
...eal cheeks with figs +++ Vegetable and chickpea couscous +...

index
BY CATEGORY

BY CATEGORY

Main dishes (continued)

VEGETARIAN

Desserts

...roth +++ Chicken cacciatore +++ Chocolate pudding cake +++ Coq... n +++ Cream of butternut squash soup with maple syrup +++ Crèm... rûlée +++ Crème caramel +++ Dahl soup +++ Date and lemon chick... jine +++ Flemish carbonnade +++ Garden ratatouille +++ Goulash... oney chicken wings +++ Jamaican-style red beans +++ Lamb nava... ...+ Lamb shanks with prunes +++ Lasagna +++ Layered "stuffe... abbage +++ Lemon pudding cake +++ Lentil stew with poached eg... ...+ Lime bavette rolls +++ Mango "jam" +++ Maple baked apples... aple and beer-braised ham +++ Maple-braised pork with parsn... nd potatoes +++ Meatloaf +++ Orange and honey turkey breast... range-braised beet salad +++ Osso buco +++ Pea soup +++ Pineapp... hicken +++ Poor man's maple pudding cake +++ Pork chili +++ Pull... ork burgers +++ Rabbit braised in red wine with pancetta +++ R... ...+ Rice pudding +++ Rouille +++ Salsa verde pork tacos +++ Salt p... ...+ Scalloped potatoes +++ Seafood and fish soup with fresh herbs... ouffléed omelette +++ Steamed salmon with fennel +++ Sticky toff... udding +++ Strawberry "jam" +++ Strawberry and rhubarb "jam"... un-dried tomato and olive strata +++ Tofu and vegetable curry... eal cheeks with figs +++ Vegetable and chickpea couscous... egetable soup +++ Vegetarian spaghetti sauce +++ Whole chicken... pple and nut cake +++ Baked beans +++ Barbecued pulled pork... eef and carrot stew +++ Beef and chickpea soup +++ Beef strogan... ...+ Beef teriyaki +++ Black bean quesadillas +++ Blue cheese dip... olognese sauce +++ Braised carrots +++ Bread pudding with ru... auce +++ Brownies +++ Cheesecake + Chicken broth +++ Chick... acciatore +++ Chocolate pudding cake +++ Coq au vin +++ Crea... f butternut squash soup with maple syrup +++ Crème brûlée... rème caramel +++ Dahl soup +++ Date and lemon chicken tajine... emish carbonnade +++ Garden ratatouille +++ Goulash +++ Hon... hicken wings +++ Jamaican-style red beans +++ Lamb navarin... amb shanks with prunes +++ Lasagna +++ Layered "stuffed" cabba... ...+ Lemon pudding cake +++ Lentil stew with poached eggs... ime bavette rolls +++ Mango "jam" +++ Maple baked apples... aple and beer-braised ham +++ Maple-braised pork with parsn... nd potatoes +++ Meatloaf +++ Orange and honey turkey breast... range-braised beet salad +++ Osso buco +++ Pea soup +++ Pineap... hicken +++ Poor man's maple pudding cake +++ Pork chili +++ Pull... ork burgers +++ Rabbit braised in red wine with pancetta +++ R... ...+ Rice pudding +++ Rouille +++ Salsa verde pork tacos +++ Salt p... ...+ Scalloped potatoes +++ Seafood and fish soup with fresh herbs... ouffléed omelette +++ Steamed salmon with fennel +++ Sticky toff... udding +++ Strawberry "jam" +++ Strawberry and rhubarb "jam"... un-dried tomato and olive strata +++ Tofu and vegetable curry... eal cheeks with figs +++ Vegetable and chickpea couscous...

index
BY CHAPTER

The everyday slow cooker

The slow cooker even in summer

index
BY CHAPTER

The vegetarian slow cooker

The slow cooker for desserts